FAMILY REUNION HANDBOOK

A guide for reunion planners

First Edition

Barbara E. Brown

Thomas Ninkovich

REUNION RESEARCH • SAN FRANCISCO • CALIFORNIA

Cover photo by Harrison Jones, Questudios, Chicago, IL.

Published by:

Reunion Research
3145 Geary Blvd. #14
San Francisco, CA 94118

Printed in Canada

Library of Congress Cataloging-in-Publication Data:

Brown, Barbara E.

Family reunion handbook: a guide for reunion planners
/Barbara E. Brown, Thomas Ninkovich. — 1st ed.
p. cm.

Includes bibliographical references and index.
ISBN 0-9610470-3-8 (pbk.): $14.95

1. Family reunions—United States—Planning. 2. Family
reunions—Canada—Planning. I. Ninkovich, Thomas.
II. Title.

GT2423.N56   1992
394.2—dc20   CIP 92-9809

IN MEMORY OF

Alex Haley

who showed us why.

DEDICATION, from Barbara Brown

To my uncle, Rev. Harold Eymann, and my aunt, Mary E. Bergthold, my father's surviving siblings. The Eymanns instilled in me the value of family and the ability to organize.

To my husband, Phil, and my son, Tor, who support me in all my endeavors.

To my mother, Marion Cracraft Eymann, who is always proud of what I do.

Acknowledgements, from Barbara Brown

Thanks to my mentor, Selma Auernheimer, who encouraged me to plan my first reunion. To my cousins, Marietta E. Carsten and Ralph Eymann, Jr., who enthusiastically supported me in organizing family and class reunions. Thanks to all who contributed ideas for this book and who filled out surveys; many of you are mentioned in the text. Additional thanks to Susan Bond, Donna Uran, Linda Irish, Eleanor Dodson, Robert T. Borreson, John E. Denhalter, Louise Schulthers, Linda Morrow, Melba Goebel, and members of the Eddy Family, especially Thomas A.C. Eddy and Doris Wright Tice.

Acknowledgements, from Tom Ninkovich

Thanks to "Coach" Tom Dougherty for his insights and help with the overall picture; to Ann Parker for editorial work and the "Destinations" chapter; to Susan Wolbarst for the "Food" chapter; to Magda Krance and Lauren Davis for help with the "Kids" chapter; to Jerry Houck for designing the Scrapbook Section; to John Holiday for looking over the chapter on "Finding People"; to John Dahle for the cartoons; and to Virginia Wright of Blue Rider Graphics, Seattle.

How to Use This Book

The information and ideas in this book have been collected over a long period of time from hundreds of different reunion planners. You will probably find much more material here than you will need for your specific reunion. To simplify things we suggest these tips:

✓ **Use a highlighting pen or colored ink to mark ideas and sections that pertain to your particular reunion.** Mark an especially important point with a paper clip. A few extra minutes spent in this way will work wonders later on. (*Note:* If this is a library book, you can order your own book with the order form in the back. Please don't mark-up library books.)

✓ For a **complete list of the services** Reunion Research provides and an updated price list, please send for our catalog. Also see pages 213–16.

The **Appendix** lists all sources and resources mentioned in the text plus additional information that may be useful.

This book is updated with each printing. Much new and revised information is included. If this book is more than three years old (check date in front), consider getting an updated copy. If you have problems contacting any of the sources, businesses, or organizations listed, please write to us for updated information. Send a self-addressed, stamped envelope with your request.

Please Help!

The information in this book came from people like you. We have conducted interviews, mailed out surveys, gone to many reunions, organized our own, taken many photographs, and begged for many photographs in our quest to make this book more useful. This book is reprinted about every three years. Each edition contains more information plus new and updated resource material.

You can help. Send us any new or additional information. If it's published in our next edition, you will receive credit and can feel good about helping other reunion planners. Here's what we are looking for:

✓ New tips and ideas that aren't found in this book (preferably from your own experience).

✓ Useful criticisms of tips and ideas in this book. Try to present a good argument from your own experience.

✓ Magazine articles and newspaper clippings on the subject of: school, family, or military reunions.

✓ Addresses of businesses that have products or services for reunions.

✓ Corrections to addresses and phone numbers listed.

✓ Facilities or sites that are especially good for family reunions.

✓ Hotels or convention bureaus that specifically cater to family reunions by sponsoring special programs or tours.

✓ Other books or pamphlets on how to plan reunions.

✓ Photographs that illustrate any of the points presented in this book, or that illustrate points that you would like to see presented in future editions.

✓ Computer software that is specifically designed for reunions.

✓ Examples of memorial services and toasts given at reunions.

✓ Examples of awards and prizes not covered in the book.

✓ More material for the Scrapbook Section.

"....of all the nostalgias that haunt the human heart, the greatest of them all is an everlasting longing to bring what is youngest home to what is oldest."

—*Laurens van der Post*

"....the effect of order within the family is to create an influence that brings order into the world."   —*I Ching*

CONTENTS

OLD ECHOES from a FAMILY REUNION

Around the festive board, old faces missed
Replace themselves with new ones: likeness-kissed —
The sweetness of a certain curve of cheek;
The tone of voice when one is heard to speak;
The grave regard of granite-colored eyes
Repeat the portraits on the wall; surprise
The senses with a spurt of memory
That answers every questing enquiry,
As potent as the scent of a pressed rose!
How does a child reflect an aunt's repose,
Who never knew her mentor, long at rest,
But read her yellowed diary, frightened lest
The pages crumble in her smooth young hand?
A boy who knew not his ancestral land
Still bears the stamp of mountains and fjords;
The music's in his bones — the primal chords.
All that we have become, we owe the old
Who went before — their warmth would pierce the cold
Of this year's end and grey December day,
Where past has more than present words to say.

— Jane Carpenter

Foreword

No other institution in our society has more influence on the lives of all its members than the family. As the provider of nurture and socialization, it is the basis of individual well-being. It remains the unique source of identity, and emotional satisfactions that meet basic human needs.

As society changes, the ways in which we relate and convey the family functions also change. The family reunion can be a vehicle for carrying out the extended family functions that many of us experienced when families lived closer together and in the same neighborhoods. Family reunions offer a potential structure for enhancing and maintaining the vitality and viability of the extended family concept.

Reunions have several benefits. Through the activities that are planned, reunions transmit values, foster greater communication between family members, provide a great deal of education, and recognize the talents and role models within the family. A most important factor is the confirmation of identity and sense of belonging that occurs. Families grow and develop as the extended family members play out traditional roles which have been diminished in a mobile society.

Families may not usually gather with these benefits in mind. But a well planned reunion inadvertently makes them happen. Thus the family reunion is to be encouraged and can help us strengthen our extended family.

—Ione Dugger Vargus, Ph.D.
   Acting Vice-Provost and
      Chair, Family Reunion Institute
   Temple University, Philadelphia

Introduction

More and more people are finding family reunions assuming an important role in their lives. As well as being joyous events, reunions can be rewarding in ways that modern day society seems to have lost.

For untold years, everything available to a person was to be found within a few miles and among a few people. We still long for this simple and effective type of social structure. It's no accident that family reunions awaken strong feelings of need and potential fulfillment. They provide a means of harkening back to times gone by, when aunts and uncles and grandparents were part of the fabric of everyday life, dispensing lore and psychology as required. This kind of contact is still needed, but the ways of providing it have slowly disappeared. The extended family is gone. The nuclear family is less common; a child is lucky to have two parents these days. Aunts, uncles, and grandparents are visited infrequently, if at all. The family reunion is a way of recapturing some of the warmth and nurturing of older times.

     *   *   *   *   *

That initial phone call may be hesitant, just as the initial invitation may be hurriedly written. And the first reunion may be nothing more than a barbeque in Grandma's back yard. However, your first effort may eventually become more elaborate. The next reunion may be in a banquet room of a hotel. And a few more down the line may find you at a beautiful state park.

More importantly, your reunion can grow in terms of being intellectually stimulating and emotionally rewarding. In many instances, family members will find a reunion psychologically supportive as well.

You may discover new friends among those family members taken for granted all these years. That's what happened to Linda Ludwig Irish. She found the most memorable part of the Ludwig Family Reunion as being "The way we all seemed to fit together. For some of us, this was the first time we ever met, yet we seemed to be old friends."

Family reunions can be interesting, revealing, and mentally stimulating. A lot can be learned, both *about* the family and *from* the family. As Linda points out, "With the family spread all over the country like it is today, it's more important than ever to keep the family reunion tradition. So much can be learned at these gatherings about one's family."

You may find some really strong people in your family, people who silently and consistently make a difference in the world in their own quiet way. You may discover new meaning in the old saying, "Mighty oaks from little acorns grow."

Family reunions can also provide an historical "anchor," a sense of historical continuence, especially when several generations—ranging from great-grandparents to little babies—are present. With the divorce rate so high and so many single-parent homes, family reunions can provide some needed stability within our relatively rootless society. In essence, a family reunion can make one feel less alone in a society seemingly characterized by a lack of familial cohesiveness. Ronald Eddy Austin singled this out as one of the rewards of the Eddy Family Reunion: "(It) gives you a sense of your place in history...a sense of belonging to a larger extended family, which in turn, is part of the world family." Elizabeth Jones echoed this feeling when describing her family's reunion: "(It) made me think about where we all come from and where we are going."

Big or small, we encourage you to begin....to start planning your family reunion. The rewards are great. You'll know just how great when that long-lost favorite cousin walks through the door or when your kids ask expectantly when the next reunion is going to be.

—Tom Ninkovich
Miramonte, CA

CHAPTER 1

Early Decisions:
First Things First

*Types of Reunions – When to Circle the Calendar – How Often
Should You Have a Reunion? – How Long Should It Last? –
Reunion Size – Where, Oh Where? – Site-Choosing Check List –
Banquet Room Check List – Negotiating/Contracts.*

Types of Reunions

Reunions, like family members, come in all shapes and
sizes. The first task of those planning a reunion is to decide
what kind to have. It can be a huge, joyous gathering or a
small, low key event. It can last for several hours or several
days. It can be held on the same weekend every year or once
every five years. It can be in Grandma's back yard, at a dude
ranch, or in a large hotel. Some reunions return to the same
spot each time. Others move around.

You can start with a small, simple reunion and work up to
a big, expensive one in future years. Or, more realistically, a
big, expensive reunion can be a once-in-a-lifetime event that

could be announced years in advance so that everyone has
time to plan and save.

One of the points this book emphasizes is that different
types of reunions add variety and create interest. This is especially helpful if your annual reunion has reached the "boring"
stage, as many of them do. But, fortunately, boring reunions
can be changed to interesting ones without throwing money at
them, as we shall see.

Of course, no matter what kind of reunion you choose to
have, the focus is on bringing the family together to celebrate
their roots and to get to know each other better.

Your first consideration is the family members themselves—their ages, agility, disabilities, where they live, their
financial resources, and who is to be included. If everyone is to
be included—young, very old, disabled, rich, poor, out-of-
towners, and locals—then the most popular type of reunion is
a picnic or barbeque in a city or state park. That's because
such a reunion tends to be the cheapest and easiest to plan.
However, other options are possible that don't involve too
much more expenditure of time and money—and offer variety
and interest as well.

If you would like something other than the usual picnic or barbeque, consider your family's background and interests when choosing the kind of reunion. Ask yourself, what is unique about my family? Do family members have interests in common? If they do, plan your reunion to include one or more of these interests. For example, if your family likes outdoor activity, plan a reunion at a guest ranch, or plan to camp, backpack, or boat. Or plan a reunion around the most popular family sport; it may be on the water, the ski slopes, or the baseball diamond.

If the family interests are more intellectual, a reunion near a Shakespeare festival, a group of art galleries, or an archaeological dig could be a great experience. Another family might want a catered event in a fancy resort with evening entertainment. If the family is interested in exploring its roots, it could meet near the old family homestead, tour the hometown area, travel to the family homeland, do genealogical research, or restore together the family cemetery or the old family home. Another family might be ecology oriented and want a reunion focused on helping the environment in some way, such as building or restoring a trail, helping students catalog insects, or studying glaciers.

We found many families around the country creating reunions based on shared interests. The Hudson Family patterned their reunion after a country fair. This creative family displayed its crafts, art, and collections, including the work of the children. They held classes during the event to stimulate interest in each individual craft or art. Relatives demonstrated, among other crafts, rattlesnake skin-tanning and wood-root clock making. These classes created an appreciation for the talents of family members and passed on skills that might have been lost. Food booths and games added fun, challenge, and excitement to the festive fair atmosphere.

Another family visited the community where the great-grandparents were buried, took pictures in the cemetery, and looked up family obituaries on microfilm in the local library to add to the family genealogical information.

Since the widely-scattered Eymann Family grew up with camping in their blood, it seemed only natural to gather for a campout reunion. The first one was held on a cattle ranch in the Sierra foothills of California. The family arranged their tents and RV's around a central campfire, covered-wagon style. Ranging in age from three to 80, the Eymann's hiked, panned for gold, and exchanged news as they cooked family favorites on their camp stoves. The most treasured times were spent around evening campfires where everyone sang favorite songs and listened to both true and "tall" tales of the family's past.

As mentioned before, many families have a picnic reunion in a nearby park. This type of reunion, too, can be made interesting and fun by planning special events. The Kuhlmann Family met one year in Faust County Park, Missouri. Their picnic was catered by friends, leaving family members free to enjoy each other's company. The young people played ball, some older folks played cards, but most enjoyed just visiting and getting acquainted.

Other possibilities:

✓ join a tour (historical, sightseeing, religious, environmental)

✓ stay at a guest ranch

✓ lose weight at a spa

✓ go on a cattle drive, pan for gold, join a wagon train

✓ entertain the kids at Disneyland, Disneyworld, or Sea World

✓ experience the wilderness by rafting down a river, backpacking, or camping out

✓ live in a Native American village

✓ rent a houseboat on a lake

✓ watch whales

✓ take a riverboat cruise

✓ go on a bicycle or motorcycle trip

✓ enroll in a summer class at an Elderhostel or at the Smithsonian

✓ visit a national, state, or historical park

✓ bareboat in the Caribbean or in the San Juan Islands

✓ take a cruise to Alaska, Mexico, Hawaii, or up the St. Lawrence River

✓ go windjamming

✓ gather at a church retreat

✓ attend a YMCA family camp

✓ take a train ride coast to coast

✓ attend the Olympics or World's Fair

✓ meet at Ellis Island

The possibilities are endless. See the special "Scrapbook Section" in the back and Chapter 11 for more ideas.

When to Circle the Calendar

Certain decisions about the reunion must be made at least 8 months to a year ahead—in some cases, as much as 2 years ahead. *The most important decision is to set the date* so that family members can put it on their calendars before planning vacations. The year-end holidays can be a good time to communicate about a reunion planned for the following summer. Sending an announcement in your annual holiday cards can save on a separate mailer. However, this means the committee must meet *before* then to determine the date, location, and type of reunion. Elaborate plans such as renting a popular resort may require two or three years of advance planning time. Even some small, local facilities may need to be reserved a year in advance. Start early!

Most family reunions are held between June and September because the weather is better, travel is easier, school is out, and summer is the traditional time for vacations. However, some organizers are starting to take advantage of the "value" or "off" seasons in different parts of the country, which include April-May and October-November. These are the times of low tourism when accommodations and airline rates tend to be lower. A little-known fact is that, in many areas, Memorial Day, the Fourth of July, and Labor Day are also "off" seasons. Accommodations that are normally full with business trade can be relatively empty during the holidays. Holiday weekends in these areas are perfect for multi-day reunions. Good examples are Chicago, Washington DC, and New York City.

Except in ski areas, the most extensive "off" season of all takes place between December and February. However, weather and travel conditions (especially for driving) can be discouraging. For much of this time, school is still in session, and areas with good weather, like Miami and Phoenix, are having booming business and rates are actually at their highest.

Thanksgiving or year-end holidays can be a good time for some small family reunions close to home. However, this rarely works for large groups because a reunion at this time may not be the first priority for many of the people invited.

A reunion date can also be chosen because of a family milestone or special day, such as:

✓ a silver or golden wedding anniversary.

✓ a grandparent's or elder's birthday.

✓ an ancestor's birthday or date of immigration.

✓ a christening or baptism.

✓ a wedding or graduation.

✓ the anniversary of the date the ancestors opened their first business or bought their first farm.

✓ a retirement party.

✓ a special ethnic or religious holiday.

Many families set a reunion date they can count on from year to year, such as the "second Saturday in August," and they always have their reunion at this time. The reunion may not be held every year, but when it *is* held everyone knows when it will be.

By the way, it's important to set a date for your reunion and *stick to it*. There will always be conflicts for someone, but changing the date will only create conflicts for others. If there are certain family members who *must* be included, contact them before setting the date.

How Often Should You Have Reunions?

A successful first-time family reunion is actually very easy to pull off. You don't have to concern yourself with nonstop activities and programs because just being together will inspire activity and communication. All you need is a comfortable place where people can talk and children can play. These first-time reunions often turn out so well that family members ask for reunions every year. The first two or three are fine, but then interest and attendance dwindles and the reunion "blahs" begin.

The most often-heard complaint from experienced reunion planners is that annual reunions quickly become boring; the original "spark" is no longer there. There are two ways to deal with this: One is to put some years between your reunions, so that the old "yearning" comes back. The other is to show folks a really good time, especially the kids (see Chapter 9). Of course, a combination of the two is even better.

Annual reunions require the effort of a "primary mover" with lots of enthusiasm. If you lack this enthusiasm year after year, you should seriously consider putting 3 to 5 years between your reunions. It will do wonders for the "reunion morale" of your group, and you may find your own interest returning as well.

How Long Should It Last?

Family reunions vary in length from an afternoon to 3 or more days. A general rule is that the farther people must travel, the longer the reunion should last. An afternoon may not be long enough to justify the time and expense of a long trip.

The average length of a small reunion is one very full day. Larger reunions last two and three days. Four days may be a bit too long. You don't want it too short, but too long is worse. Your next reunion will benefit if you "leave them wanting more."

Reunion Size

If you have not had reunions before, one of the tricky aspects is determining how many will attend. The number affects the size of facility you will need and the cost per person. An early survey should be mailed stating the projected date, place, tentative plans, and possible costs, and requesting a response by a certain date. The response should indicate who and how many hope to attend. With this information, the committee can rent a facility and determine actual costs per person. (See Chapter 5 for more suggestions about what to include in mailers and surveys.)

Another consideration is how many family members to invite. If your family is small, there's no problem—invite them all. If it's large with many branches, the question is where to draw the line. If in doubt, start small and expand later. A reunion for 20 people is a lot different than a reunion for 200. Most people will tell you that the small "first time" reunions are the best anyway.

Then if your group has the interest and resources for a larger reunion next time, go for it. But always choose a group size that you feel comfortable managing. Having too many people to coordinate may greatly diminish your interest in organizing the next reunion. And remember, it's difficult to reduce the size of your reunion by leaving out family branches that have been previously included.

Some years you could hold *mini-reunions.* For example, one year all the younger cousins could hire a pack station to take them into the Rockies for a week of fly fishing and hiking. Another year the older generation might travel to visit the family homeland. Yet another year the whole clan may get together and share the adventures from these mini-reunions, showing slides and videos, and sharing stories. A reunion for everyone could be held near those who, because of age or disability, couldn't participate in the more active reunions. In this way, the elderly or disabled can share vicariously in the adventures of their clan. Everyone is included and family ties are strengthened.

Where, Oh Where?

Site selection is one of the most important early decisions because it's going to affect *other* decisions. Budgetwise, you won't even know what to charge until you settle on a site. And you certainly can't send out invitations until you know where the reunion is going to be.

Many separate factors are involved in choosing a site, such as the time of ycar you intend to meet, the length of the reunion, and how easy it is to get there. But the most important factor of all is the type of reunion which, in turn, should be based on the interests of your group. If it's a rafting trip, you need to pick the river. If it's a picnic in the park, the best location may be determined by its proximity to the greatest number of family members. If it's a cruise, you need to pick the destination.

Some groups opt for the convenience of a full-service hotel located near a large metropolitan airport. The hotel sales manager will gladly explain the attractions and conveniences of the particular hotel and area. Most hotels offer special group rates, and many can take care of some of the details for you including kid's programs, signs, photography, music, decorations, tours, etc.

You could rent meeting and banquet rooms that are located near, but completely separate from, your accommodations. For example, you could book a motel, then use a nearby community center or park for meals and program, and hire a caterer to serve the meals. This arrangement can certainly save money on sleeping rooms (motels with meeting facilities tend to be more expensive), and possibly on the meeting/banquet rooms, too. Do your homework; make some comparisons.

Of course, many large restaurants have banquet rooms. And, depending on your group's size, this may be ideal if the restaurant is near good accommodations and there is space (especially outdoors) for the kids to play. This can also work well if your group has few children.

Some colleges and private schools host multi-day reunions in the summer months by renting out dormitory rooms and allowing access to their cafeteria and sports facilities. Dude ranches and resorts often have group plans. Many lakes and parks provide group camping and RV areas.

Some horse racing tracks cater to reunions. Longacres, a racetrack near Seattle, often accommodates up to four reunions per day during the summer racing season. Such places usually require that you purchase the meal from them, rather than hire your own caterer.

Of course, a reunion is easier to plan if it's near your home. However, don't let this fact prevent you from eventually ranging farther afield. There are many interesting opportunities awaiting your family out there. Remember, when you *do* choose a distant location, having a family member or "helper" who lives somewhere near the chosen site is always a great advantage.

Some families enjoy taking turns hosting a reunion in their hometown or state. This can add interest to the reunion and everyone learns more about the host family. However, if the host family lives "off the beaten track" or at a great distance from the rest of the family, such an arrangement could be expensive for those who must travel. But, an "out of the way" reunion could be held occasionally.

To get the best attendance at a first-time reunion, it's important to pick a location that is centrally located to those invited. Still, you probably won't be able to please everyone. If finances are a problem, family members might pitch-in to help finance the trip for older family members on fixed incomes or others who could not afford the trip otherwise.

You may like to host a reunion, but feel that your hometown isn't very interesting. Check with your local Chamber of Commerce to see what they publicize to attract people to your area; locals are often unaware of this information. Touring a local gallery, park, or factory, though familiar to you, might be great fun for others.

Your Site-Choosing Check List

Photocopy this list to use as a guide when picking a site. You can add other items that pertain to your individual situation. *If you have a particular interest in children's activities, see the site selection list in Chapter 9.*

✓ Facilities in suburban or rural areas surrounding a large city are usually more inexpensive than those located in downtown areas. Get a map of the area and write or call the Chambers of Commerce in some of the smaller outlying towns to find out what accommodations and facilities are available.

✓ Find out if convenient, inexpensive transportation exists between the airport or train station and where people will be staying. Is there access to public transportation? Is there a shuttle service?

✓ Ask each facility manager you contact for the names and phone numbers of other family reunions or similar events that have recently used the facility. Call these people for their opinions and suggestions; while you are at it, get referrals from them for suppliers you may need, such as photographers, musicians, florists, etc.

✓ If a member of your group lives in the area, have them check each potential facility in person. Provide them with this list.

✓ Find out when the facility's "off" season occurs (the time when rates are lowest).

✓ Ask if a deposit is required. When it is due? The refunding policy. Does the deposit cover "cancellation" only or does it also include "breakage and damage"?

✓ Always ask what "freebies" are available. Every facility has its own rules in this regard. The most common "freebie" at a hotel is a free sleeping room for so many paid rooms (the usual ratios are 1–40 or 1–50).

✓ Watch for extra costs. A general meeting room, doughnuts and coffee, audio-visual equipment, extra tables and chairs, etc., can range from being free to costing much more than they are worth. Discuss every detail with the manager. With a little persuasion, some of the above items might be tossed in free.

✓ Are tables and chairs available for registration? Tables and bulletin boards for memorabilia? Are there moveable chalk boards or placards for announcements and signs? Is there a charge for these?

✓ What is the "smoking/nonsmoking" policy? Are there "no smoking" sleeping rooms?

✓ If needed, is there wheelchair access?

✓ Are there nearby RV and camper accommodations?

✓ Is there ample parking? Is it free? Is there a public lot nearby? Handicapped parking?

✓ Always have the facility prepare a contract with all details covered. Then you can be assured that you both agree.

✓ Ask the facility to provide you with a map of the surrounding area, including the airport and train station, and written driving directions to the site (for your mailers).

Your Banquet Room Check List

If you intend to rent a banquet room, here are some specific things to watch for:

✓ How many people can the room accommodate? Are there different rooms to choose from? Ask for a floor plan of the room showing how they intend to set it up (tables, chairs, etc.).

✓ What are the "hours of access" to the room? When is closing time?

✓ What is the time-table for guaranteeing the "meal count" (usually 48 hours before the event for the minimum count, 24 hours for the final count)? What about people who show up unannounced? What is the "overset" (percentage over the final meal count that can be served—usually 5%)?

✓ Can the room be decorated? What time can you start? What are the limitations? Can you use masking tape or thumb tacks? Who removes the decorations?

✓ Can you attend a function to see the facility "in action"? Can you sample the food? (Offer to be discreet when you observe and offer to pay for the food.)

✓ Can you bring your own wine for a toast? Are wine glasses available? (Don't forget a corkscrew and ice bucket.)

✓ Is there a public address system? Who sets it up? Is there a stage? A lecturn or podium?

✓ Is there a slide or movie projector and screen? Are there extra bulbs? Extension cords? Table for projector? VCR and monitor? Duct tape to secure extension cords to the floor?

Call or write the Convention and Visitors Bureau or Chamber of Commerce in any given area for a list of facilities and other services. It's handy to have a telephone book of your chosen city. Get both white and yellow pages, if they are separated (as with most large cities). Ask a hotel or the Convention Bureau if they can send these to you. Otherwise, see the Appendix for a source for any phone book in the country.

Negotiating and Contracts

We present here only the fundamentals of "negotiating and contracts," mostly for the benefit of large reunion groups that are using the services of a hotel or resort. For a more thorough discussion on the subject, we refer you to Chapter 3 of *Military Reunion Handbook* (see p. 214).

Negotiating. It's true that large groups have more bargaining power than small groups when it comes to negotiating. That's the nature of the game. But don't think you are too small to negotiate successfully. Negotiating will work to some extent regardless of your size.

Most people don't even realize they can negotiate terms and rates with hotels and resorts. But not doing so is equivalent to paying the sticker price for a new car. Most reunion planners, especially first-timers, *do* pay more than necessary, or fail to get some extras that could be their's for the asking.

So how do you prepare to negotiate? Proper negotiating allows both parties to win and to look good. It's important to be well prepared. This involves:

✓ Identifying the needs and desires of your group.

✓ Knowing the economic value of your reunion.

✓ Understanding the hotel/resort's position.

✓ Knowing what is negotiable.

✓ Comparing rates with other facilities.

Of course, you should always negotiate a "group room rate." But you should also ask for some complimentary items. If you don't ask, they won't be offered. While you may not get something for free, you may get some things at a reduced rate. The list below will give you an idea of what may be available.

But remember, getting one or more of these items depends on how the hotel views the economic value of your business. If this is your first reunion, or if your reunion is very small, don't expect to get all or even most of these items.

Some negotiable items:

✓ A complimentary welcoming reception.

✓ One free room for every 40 or 50 sold is standard, but maybe you can do better.

✓ Free storage for supplies shipped in advance.

✓ Free recreational activities.

✓ Complimentary suite for your hospitality room.

✓ Suite for the price of a regular room.

✓ Meeting room.

✓ Audio/visual equipment.

✓ Free parking.

✓ Early check-in, late check-out.

✓ Use of hotel limo or bus.

✓ Signs for your registration area.

✓ Free meal or sleeping room to use as door or raffle prize.

✓ Flowers and table decorations.

Contracts. Once you have finished negotiating, you should receive a written contract from the sales manager. This is a very important document, and once signed, is legally binding on both parties.

A good contract or letter of agreement is a road map spelling out the responsibilities of both parties, and ensures that they will meet their obligations. It does not have to be in fancy legalese, but don't use unclear words in the contract such as "may" or "a reasonable amount." Once you sign it, send it back by certified mail.

One word of caution: Most contracts are made up by the hotel and usually benefit the hotel. Some of the small points that were verbally agreed upon during negotiations may not be included. Read it all very carefully before signing. Do not take anything for granted, and do not be pushed into signing quickly. Everything that you agreed to should be listed, no matter how small. If items must be added to the contract, spell them out very carefully and ask the hotel to do the re-writing. Small items can be written in by hand, and should be initialed and dated.

The following list is a guide for checking your contract:

✓ Accommodations: types of rooms and beds, total number of rooms blocked, check-in/check-out dates and times, complimentary rooms, extended stays/early arrivals, suites, reservation cut-off dates.

✓ Finances: deposits (how much and when?), master billing accounts (when due?), billing arrangements, authorized signatures, taxes, built-in gratuity.

✓ Transportation.

✓ Meeting space.

✓ Food and beverage (common: 50% due 30 days prior, balance due 7 days prior).

✓ Equipment, signs, services.

✓ Parking.

✓ Renovation/construction inconvenience.

✓ Change of ownership/management agreements.

✓ Termination/cancellation agreements (individual room cancellation charges, if any, should not be borne by the group; there should not be an event cancellation charge other than loss of deposit).

✓ Procedure if over-booked.

✓ Extras agreed upon during negotiations.

CHAPTER 2

Getting Organized: Committees/Meetings

*Beginnings – Committees – Meetings – Tips for Committee
Leaders – Seed Money – That Special Idea – Areas of
Responsibility.*

Beginnings

The first family reunion is usually organized by the person
or family who originally has the idea. Someone starts wonder-
ing about a cousin they used to spend summers with as a kid
or wishing their children knew more about their roots. So they
call their cousin and discover that he or she, too, has been
thinking about the rest of the clan. One of them says, "Let's get
together" and the first step towards a family reunion has been
taken.

At least one enthusiastic person who can get things done is
the key to successful reunion organization. This person usually has the time, energy, creativity, and organizational abilities
to do the necessary planning and arranging. However, if this
doesn't describe you, don't worry; maybe you are just the

catalyst. Many reunions would not happen at all if it were not for someone getting the idea started. Show this book to others in your family; maybe your spark will take flame.

Committees

If your group stays small, one person may be all you need for leadership. However, in some families, especially if reunion

interest increases, other forms of leadership may evolve in order to handle all the work.

Most reunion planning eventually becomes a team effort; in other words, committees are formed to share the work. The committee members may all be from one family or different families. Family branches can take turns being in charge from year to year. Committee heads can be chosen and each one has helpers or teams of helpers who do different tasks. In fact, the more family members who can be involved, the more interest is generated for attending the reunion.

In large families with lots of branches, teams can be organized to handle special concerns within their own families, such as dietary needs and mobility problems. Each team has a liaison on the main committee. Different family branches can be in charge of specific details, such as lodging, food, events, childcare, cleanup, etc.

Larger or experienced families often have a Reunion Committee headed by a

Reunion Chairperson. These committees may also have a Site Coordinator who is chosen because he or she lives near the reunion site. It's this person's job to be the liaison between the Reunion Committee and the local suppliers (the people and businesses providing goods and services for the reunion). If subsequent reunions are held in different locations, then the Site Coordinator changes accordingly. In many cases, the person is picked first, and then the site is chosen near where that person lives.

Meetings

With family reunions, it can be difficult for a committee to meet, given the fact that members are likely to be scattered around the country. Your meetings may have to take place through phone calls and letters unless some of you live within driving distance of each other. (A conference call system, called "3-way calling," is available on most residential private lines with touch-tone dialing.) It may help to schedule a meeting of the committee at the reunion site a day or two before the reunion begins. Formal family associations tend to schedule board and committee meetings before, during, or after their reunions, depending on their needs and preferences.

Your first meeting (by phone, letter, or in person) should cover picking a date, determining the type of reunion, and possibly choosing a location. Give each person something to research. One person or family could check into the availability and cost of facilities. Another person could survey family members to get ideas on the kind of reunion that would interest them. Someone else could see if there are certain dates to avoid, such as family weddings or graduations. Or perhaps organizing a reunion *around* a wedding or graduation would work best.

Tips for Committee Leaders

Suppose you are a committee chairperson; volunteers have been found, jobs and authority have been delegated, and things are getting done. At this point, your job *begins!* Once assignments have been agreed upon, you must follow up. After all, the main role of a committee leader is to see that all the little details get done. Make sure people are doing what they said they would do, and within the time-frame agreed upon. Whatever you do, don't neglect your job or expect that people will maintain a high level of enthusiasm and commitment over the many months it takes to produce a successful reunion. *You must provide leadership*—and that may include keeping people motivated.

In the initial flush of excitement, some people may take on more than they can handle. Some have a hard time saying no. Several weeks down the line they may find themselves with a crucial job and no time to do it. However, *someone* has to do it. If you are keeping track of your volunteers, catch the over-committed ones before it's too late and re-assign some of their work to others.

Don't be tempted to take on their tasks yourself unless it is absolutely necessary. You want to make it to the reunion without becoming terminally stressed out. Since you can't do everything, keep everyone on track doing "their thing."

It's important that the people assigned to certain tasks understand why, when, and how their tasks are to be accomplished. Since people can forget, give each volunteer a check list of duties. Creating this list and going over it is time well spent. Understanding and accomplishment go hand in hand. (See next page for a list of the various responsibilities.)

Seed Money

(See Chapter 3 for more information on finances.)

While you are getting the ball rolling, who is paying for phone calls, photocopying, postage, envelopes, etc.? At first *you* may have to cover expenses, but eventually the costs must be shared among your family members. *Start asking for donations or dues right away* and keep accurate records. Make requests through your mailers or a few strategic phone calls. A good way to convince people of your trustworthiness is to send out a financial report. Also, ask the most interested people to pay their reunion fees ahead of time. By the time the reunion gets close, there should be enough seed money for mailing, phone calls, office supplies, and a deposit to hold the facility.

If, for some reason, the reunion never gets off the ground, you should still reimburse yourself from these funds before returning the remainder. Unless you clearly state otherwise, however, this should be a break-even situation; you should not profit from it or charge for your labor.

That Special Idea

Occasionally someone will come up with a really great idea, but can't convince others on the committee to go along with it. Committees are notoriously conservative because they must compromise; this can really take the "spark" out of an excellent idea. If someone in your group is really committed to an idea, but can't get others to see their viewpoint, perhaps that person should be allowed to do the project by themselves, or with the help of a few people of their own choosing. This approach could work well if the project only covers a particular part of the reunion, such as decorations, a newsletter, or a portion of the program, *and* if it doesn't cost too much.

Areas of Responsibility

Here is a list of various responsibilities that can be delegated. They can be assigned to individuals or sub-committees. Some can be combined; some may not pertain to your reunion.

To do before the reunion (or year-around, if you are an on-going group):

✓ Locating family members
✓ Registration by mail
✓ Maintaining the mailing list
✓ Budgeting/finances
✓ Bookkeeping/bank account
✓ Fund-raising

✓ Writing newsletters and mailers

✓ Mailing

✓ Handling information: answering questions, receiving information on missing family members, receiving donations, etc.

✓ Keeping historical data: scrapbooks, old movies, videos, mementos, family history, genealogy, oral history, etc.

✓ Conducting surveys/compiling statistics

To do at the reunion:

✓ Food/beverage: organizing meals, refreshments

✓ Music: band/DJ/tapes

✓ Program

✓ Extra events: tours, church service, memorial service, sports events, etc.

✓ Public address system, audio-visual equipment

✓ Decorations

✓ Photography

✓ Memory book

✓ Video

✓ Children's activities

✓ Adult activities

✓ Registration desk

✓ Name tags/badges/signs

✓ Door prizes

✓ Housing/RV arrangements

✓ Parking

✓ Selection and presentation of gifts, scholarships, or special awards

✓ Family store/merchandise

✓ Fund-raising

✓ Set-up/clean-up

CHAPTER 3

Money and Finances

Who's in Charge? – The Budget – Sources of Income – Figuring Expenses – Setting the Rates – Refunding Policy – Raising $$$ – The Family Store – Planned Fund-Raisers – Emergency Fund Raisers – Other Fund-Raising Ideas – Underwriter Certificates – Take-Home Gifts – Tickets – Bank Accounts – Bookkeeping – Saving $$$ – Keep a Financial History.

Who's in Charge of Finances?

If your reunion is small, perhaps you can do everything and handle the money, too. However, as your reunion gets larger, you may need help. The two basic financial areas are "money management" and "bookkeeping." If you can find a family member with both these abilities—great! If not, or if one person simply doesn't have the time to do both, then divide up these responsibilities. Since all well-managed households have such people, you shouldn't have to look too far to find them. In family associations, this structure may evolve into a Finance Committee with the treasurer as chairperson.

The Budget

Some reunion planners assume that the finances will take care of themselves. However, creating a budget, collecting funds, and using these funds appropriately are important parts of a successful reunion.

When creating a budget, here are two important tips to remember:

1. Be as thorough as possible. Anything you leave out or miscalculate can cause a short-fall. These oversights can come back to "haunt" you in some embarassing ways, such as asking reunion members to kick in more money at the last minute.

2. Miscalculations *can* be made, especially by those with little or no experience. Add a "fudge" factor of about 10% to help off-set such mistakes. This factor can be adjusted (hopefully, reduced) with experience.

Sources of income. Sources of income for your reunion will normally come from the following:

✓ Registration fees and/or dues
✓ Ticket sales for meals and tours
✓ Donations
✓ Advertising in, or subscriptions to, your family newsletter
✓ Fund-raisers
✓ Sale of merchandise, family histories, group photos, memory books, videos, etc.

Figuring expenses. When preparing a budget, figuring expenses is of great importance. Remember, though, that some expenses are paid for directly by the attendees. For example, the reunion fund should not pay for:

– hotel rooms or travel (exception: honored guests).
– tours or cruises (in most cases).
– meals not included in the program.

It's easy to overlook an item in calculating the total cost of a reunion. Below is a list of basic items you can use as a guide. Most of these items are discussed separately and at length elsewhere in this book.

List of reunion expenses:

✓ reimbursing out-of-pocket costs incurred up to the time a reunion fund is created (phone calls, mailings, expense of finding people, deposits, stationery, office supplies, etc.)

✓ food and beverage

✓ discrepancies in meal counts at pre-paid meals, discrepancies in tour counts, etc. (If your count is off by more than the agreed upon amount, you are responsible.)

✓ coffee/refreshment breaks, snacks

✓ wine or after dinner drinks for toasts

✓ music/entertainment

✓ photography/videography

✓ decorations (room, table, banners, flags, flowers, etc.)

✓ cost of mailers (calculated from number of mailings, how many pieces in each mailing, how much postage per piece, printing or copying costs, envelopes, rubber stamps, etc.)

✓ printing of programs, invitations, etc.

✓ signs/placards

✓ shipping (of items too large or awkward to transport any other way)

✓ awards/door prizes

✓ name tags

✓ fund-raising items (for auction or raffle)

✓ mementos (personalized take-home gifts)

✓ long-distance phone calls

✓ flowers or wreaths for memorial service

✓ taxes

✓ rentals (movie/slide projectors, camcorders, PA system, extra tables or chairs, podium, stage, bulletin board, punch bowls, coffee makers, utensils, canopy for shade, tents, playpens, sports equipment, wheelchairs, etc.)

✓ honored guest's rooms, meals, transportation

✓ public gift or scholarship fund

✓ funds for next reunion or on-going expenses

✓ cleanup

Expenses at hotels:

✓ hospitality suites

✓ meeting rooms

✓ tips

✓ local room-use tax

✓ rentals

Setting the rates. When figuring income, one of the questions to address is the relationship between adult and children's rates. Children's rates can be diverse; different ages pay different rates. In many public places, children twelve and older are charged adult fees. Sometimes children under a certain age are free. If you set different fees for different age children, make sure your adult rates are high enough to cover discrepancies in the costs. You may want to skip charging for children entirely and divide the costs among the adults. This is fair unless you have families with large numbers of children.

Be sure to find out from rental facilities if they are 1) charging you by-the-person, and 2) what age groups they include. If you assume, for example, they won't charge for babies, and they do charge, it could be a problem.

You could offer large families a price break to make the reunion more affordable for them. You might also consider a price break for the older members on fixed incomes. This can be facilitated by spreading the costs to other family members. All this calculating can be tricky; that's why you need someone with a good grasp of figures.

Be sensitive to the financial resources of the various families you want to include. Do not plan an event that is so expensive that members cannot attend or will have to go into debt to do so. This will not only encourage resentment, but will reduce the number attending. There is a place for fancy/expensive reunions, but they should occur only occasionally, and be announced far in advance so that people can plan accordingly (see Chapter 11).

Collecting money is an issue that causes problems for many reunions. Three problems are most common: 1) not making costs clear from the beginning, 2) not collecting enough to cover expenses, and 3) family members not paying their share.

The exact amount each family will be charged should be explained in your mailers six months or more before the event. This gives people time to cover their share. If done right, it will also give you working capital for your mailers and set-up expenses, and deposits required by facilities and caterers. You can request half (or a percentage) be paid immediately and the rest at the reunion. Or you can ask for the total ahead of time. Set a deadline for when fees are needed, and if necessary, send out friendly reminders. It's *always* easier to collect before the reunion than afterward. (Also see "Seed Money," p. 22.)

And be sure to outline the finances in the mailer or newsletter so that people can see how you arrived at the costs. Not having organized a reunion themselves, many people are totally unrealistic about what it should cost. By explaining how you arrived at the price, family members will be more understanding and willing to pay.

Refunding policy. Work out some type of refund policy. If a family cannot come because of an emergency (for instance, Johnny had an appendectomy the night before the reunion), you should refund some of the fee, but not the entire amount. Retain enough to cover mailing costs and any costs or deposits that will not be refunded to you if people do not show up (for example: meal costs). Be sure to make the refund policy clear in all your mailers.

Raising Money

Making a profit. Most one-time or first-time reunion organizers are satisfied, and consider it a job well-done, if the bank balance is zero when the whole thing is over. This is an accurate assumption because it means that it was a well-managed reunion and the attendees got the most for their money.

While breaking even is a reunion's primary financial goal, some families with on-going reunions may start aiming for a little profit. However, this isn't "profit" in the ordinary sense of the word, *i.e.*, no one is taking any of this money home. It can go toward starting the next reunion, locating more people, funding recognition awards or scholarships, memorial funds and donations to service groups, printing a family history, arranging transportation for someone who could not be at the reunion otherwise, or any number of worthy causes. Also, until you get very good at reunion finances, it could serve as your "fudge" factor.

If your group is interested in making a profit, you will need to look at some aspects of the reunion differently. With a profit-making plan, many reunion components can be for sale. Tours, photos, memory books, videos, merchandise, family histories, even the banquet meals can be bought at one price and sold to family members at another. However, there can be some risk involved. For instance, if you rent a tour bus for $300, and five people sign up for the tour at $20 per person, you've lost money.

Good financial planning is absolutely essential if you want to go this route. It's also important to explain that no one individual is making a profit—only the group is making a profit.

Some reunion organizers will not consider money making ventures or fund-raisers, feeling they involve too much time and effort for the amount of return. However, if handled properly, they can add fun and excitement to your reunion and money to your coffers, while taking only a short time to organize. There's really no reason why every reunion shouldn't stage some type of fund-raiser—unless you are allergic to extra money, a complaint we have yet to hear!

The family store. Many companies produce special mementos that can be sold at a family store: coffee mugs, steins, wine glasses, ash trays, paperweights, playing cards, pennants,

T-shirts, caps, bumperstickers, coasters, decals, tote bags, embroidered patches, badges, pens and pencils. T-shirts and baseball caps are especially popular with family reunions. Decide which of these items would interest your family and contact several suppliers to get the best prices.

Occasionally a family store is the brain child of one person or family unit that uses it to reduce their own reunion costs. However, it is more often run by the committee or family association to benefit everyone. Prices range from $1 to around $20 per item, sometimes more for items such as jackets and family crest rings. Items can be sold at the reunion and through the mail.

If merchandise offered on speculation doesn't sell, money is lost. To minimize losses, don't print the year or reunion location on family store items. Then they can be sold any year. Dated items are best used for planned fund-raising, awards, or gifts.

Other items to offer for sale can be Aunt Eleanor's family history, Cousin Barbara's latest book, a family cookbook, Grandma's wonderful raspberry jam, cousin Judy's dolls and quilts, snacks, or even donated clothing that your kids grew out of. (This is a nice place to sell or trade garments you would like to "keep in the family" that were knit by a special aunt or sewn just for your children by Grandma.)

Next to this area you can sell tickets for a pastry sale or cake walk with each family donating their favorite goodies. At a large reunion, children could set up their own flea market table to trade or sell clothes, books, and toys.

Planned fund-raisers. (For emergency fund-raisers, see the next section.) Planned fund-raising is often done by either taking orders for items or by building the price of the item directly into the registration fee, thereby selling an item to each member (they have no choice). Obviously, there is no speculation involved. Group photos or memory books can be used as planned fund-raising items if they are part of the registration fee and marked up over cost.

The secret to planned fund-raising is simple—don't gamble. A sure-fire method is to build the fund-raising cost right into the registration fee, automatically selling an item to each person who attends the reunion. There will be few complaints if the item is of high quality, reasonably priced, and you explain that part of the price of each ticket is going to a worthy cause—the reunion itself. Also, this method sells more merchandise which may put you in a lower cost-per-item category when you place your initial order. And it solves the problem of how many units to order. Choose items that aren't too exotic, too much of a novelty, or appeal only to a few people. Keep in mind that the most desirable product you are selling is the reunion ticket. A few dollars added to it won't be met with much resistance.

A few words about artwork for your personalized or imprinted items: Unless you have a professional artist in your group, let the supplier do the designing. They deal with such requests daily and their charges are usually quite reasonable (sometimes free). You should, however, send examples, photocopies, or sketches of what you envision (if anything), as well as the basic color scheme that you would like to use.

Be sure to allow enough time for ordering and delivery. Sometimes it takes two or three weeks just to get a company's brochure and delivery can take 10 weeks or more. To save time, request the brochure by phone and ask that it be sent immediately.

The best way to establish "quality control" on your items is to ask for samples of the things you are interested in before you place an order, even if you have to pay for them. The photo and description in the brochure may not exactly represent the product. In the interest of time, make this request by phone.

Be sure to get the name of the person you talk to regarding any order so any follow-up questions can be directed to this person. About a week after you send in your order, call again to make sure it's being processed. If you ask to see proofs of artwork and they are acceptable, phone or fax (rather than mail) your approval. Ten dollars in phone calls can save you weeks of time. Many companies have 800 numbers even when they are not listed in their brochures—ask!

Emergency fund-raisers. Even with a 10% "fudge factor," you may still come up short due to unforeseen expenses or insufficient income. If there is enough time before the reunion, send an appeal in the mail. Explain exactly how much you are short and what that translates to per person or per family; often you will get back even more than you asked for.

If the time frame is too tight to send out an appeal and get responses beforehand, present the problem at the reunion. But remember that reunions are famous for last minute, unannounced arrivals. If six extra people show up, at (say) $20 each, that's $120, which may make the difference. However, it's important to go to the reunion knowing exactly where you stand financially and be ready to conduct a fund-raiser, if necessary.

One solution is to create a donation jar with accompanying sign, showing expenses and how much you are short per person. Put the jar in an obvious place, announce its presence at a group meeting, and have someone circulate it occasionally. Kids often enjoy this responsibility.

The Duncan family had this problem and solved it by requesting donations for an auction. Aunt Mary brought her famous canned peaches, Cousin Edith a handmade baby quilt, Uncle Bill an heirloom rifle he could part with, and Uncle Phil one of his oil paintings. These items went on the auction block, bringing in funds far beyond their actual value. Plus everyone had great fun at this extra reunion event.

Raffles are the most common fund-raisers in emergency situations; they are quick, easy, and offer some entertainment. The concept is simple: offer something of value and sell tickets for a price that seems trivial ($1 each or 6 for $5).

Raffle items should be useful and something that everyone would want. Stay away from unusual, exotic items and anything that comes in a size. A sign like the one in Figure 1 will help advertise the raffle. Be sure to indicate how much money is needed and when the drawing will be held. Display the sign and the item(s) to be raffled in a prominent place.

A *silent auction* is actually another form of a raffle. Place the items on a table and a coffee can with slotted plastic lid next to each item. To avoid mix ups, number the item and the can with the same number. Leave the items out for several hours to allow people to place tickets in the cans of their choice. The winning tickets are drawn from each can during the program or after the main meal.

Rolls of numbered theater-type tickets can be bought at stationery or office supply stores. Double rolls are preferable and have two tickets side-by-side with the same number: one for the drawing pot and the other for the purchaser to keep. Avoid the type of tickets that require the purchaser to fill in name, address, phone number, etc. This is too time consuming at an exciting event such as a reunion and will discourage people from buying a long string of tickets.

Other fund-raising ideas. Actually, anything that is bought low and sold high can generate income. Imprinted items are the most popular, but you could also consider enlarged photographs (poster size) of your last reunion or of an old family photo, or a special family calender. Such a calendar lists family birthdays, anniversaries, and special dates.

Family cookbooks are popular with some reunions and you don't have to produce them yourself. There are cookbook printers who will do everything for you except collect the recipes (see Figure 2). These spiral-bound books contain recipes contributed by family members and are sold to friends and "back home" communities, as well as family members. They cost between $2 and $5 each to produce, depending upon size and quantity printed. The amount of profit is based on "anything the market can handle" above cost—usually around $5 per book. To sell more books, include as many recipes as possible, and be sure to credit all contributors. Everyone loves to see their names in print! Most cookbook printers have "how-to" instructions available and a free kit showing different styles of covers, dividers, and formats to choose from. See the Appendix for a list of printers, all of whom have free samples and kits for soliciting recipes.

Another popular fund-raising idea is to stage your own lottery. Lottery "scratcher" tickets are available from Scratch-It Promotions (see the Appendix). These are printed with your own messages and prizes or in a cheaper "generic" form. Rush service is available at extra cost.

Planned raffles are similar to emergency raffles, except that the prizes can be more elaborate. At family reunions, the grand

FIGURE 1. *A nice looking sign will help sell tickets.*

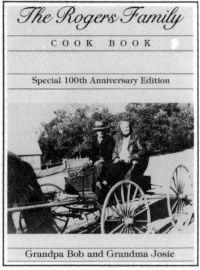

FIGURE 2. *Cookbooks are very popular fund-raisers at family reunions. A variety of covers, text styles, and formats are available. Above are shown 2 custom covers: (l) by Walter's Cookbooks, and (r) by Circulation Service. See the Appendix for addresses and additional information.*

prize can be a refund of registration fees, free transportation, a free copy of the family history, or free registration for the next reunion. A good bottle of wine makes a nice prize.

People feel like they are getting more for their money if there are several drawings for prizes instead of just one. For details on how to run a raffle, see p. 33.

Underwriter certificates (Figure 3). Here's an innovative idea submitted by Crockett A. Harrison, a member of the board of the Bartholomew Stovall Tricentennial (1984). From a mailing list of around 600, nearly 200 people bought close to 300 certificates for a total of $6000. Some people bought as many as five. Mr. Harrison explains, "In spite of our hedged promise [read certificate], we paid every note in full plus a dividend of $2 per note. This amounted to a rate of about 10% for the average time that the notes were outstanding. Most notes were endorsed over to our research fund. I insisted on the dividend and priced everything so to have the money to pay for it."

UNDERWRITER'S CERTIFICATE
FOR
BARTHOLOMEW STOVALL TRICENTENNIAL (1684-1984)

THIS CERTIFIES THAT _____ HAS ADVANCED $20.00 TO HELP DEFRAY THE EXPENSES OF PLANNING AND ORGANIZING THE BARTHOLOMEW STOVALL TRICENTENNIAL (1684-1984). THIS AMOUNT, OR AS MUCH OF IT AS FUNDS REMAINING IN THE TREASURY OF THE COMMITTEE WILL PERMIT, WILL BE REPAID AFTER ALL OBLIGATIONS HAVE BEEN SATISIFIED.

CERTIFICATE NO._____

DATE_____   _____
                                                TREASURER

FIGURE 3. This underwriter's certificate took in a lot of money for the Stovall Tricentennial reunion (1984).

Take-Home Gifts

Take-home gifts are given to those attending as a good-will gesture. They can be some of the same items found in the family store, but the expense is planned and the gift is a surprise. The price is usually covered by the registration fee and items are not marked up. A gift of good quality will be appreciated and valued as a reunion remembrance. Some items may become keepsakes and handed down within the family, generation after generation.

It's important that take-home gifts be of high quality. A cheap looking item will draw complaints ("waste of money"), while a high quality item will receive compliments. Most re-unions choose items that range in price from $3 to $10. Some possibilities are paperweights, wine glasses, cups or mugs, coasters, key rings, etc.

The Matter of Tickets

At some point you will be collecting registration fees by mail. It may seem to be a good business practice to indicate that a financial transaction has taken place by sending out receipts or tickets. However, tickets cost money to print or buy; addressing and mailing envelopes to send them takes more time and money.

An easier method is to indicate on all correspondence:

> NO TICKETS WILL BE SENT—RECEIPT OF
> YOUR CHECK RESERVES YOUR SPACE.

For this method, you *must* have a list of those who pre-registered, plus the bookkeeping records, available at the reunion's registration desk.

Another method is to state on all correspondence:

> YOUR CANCELLED CHECK SERVES AS YOUR TICKET.

However we don't recommend this method for the following reasons: 1) Most people will forget to bring their cancelled check, 2) Some people won't have their checks because some checking accounts are set up so that cancelled checks are not returned except by request, and 3) A late payment may not clear the bank in time for the cancelled check to be returned.

Bank Accounts

It's important to set up a *reunion checking account*. This step eliminates having your personal finances mixed with reunion finances. Your monthly statement is a legal and permanent record of your transactions and anyone who might question your finances can see the results in black and white (and sometimes red). Instead of having checks made out to you, they should be made out to the name of your family group. Many banks have a policy allowing free checking accounts for temporary events such as one-time reunions, but you will need to ask the bank manager about this. To get the best rate, phone several banks to check their policies.

Some families require two signatures on the reunion checking account. However, getting the other signature on each check can be time consuming and awkward. For instance, what if the other person goes on summer vacation just when you must pay the printer? A more realistic approach is to have two or three people able to make withdrawals with just one signature required. Of course, with formal family organizations the treasurer will sign checks.

When the reunion is over, and you are sure all the checks have cleared the bank, you can put any leftover money into a savings account to gain interest until the next reunion. This is a good time to have two signatures required for withdrawal.

When dealing with banks, the sticky part comes—if you are an informal group—with interest-bearing accounts (checking or savings). Technically, the federal government requires that someone be responsible for paying taxes on the earned interest. This means the bank may ask for a social security number and the person with that number must treat the interest from the account as part of his or her personal income. Obviously, some people may be reluctant to do this. With a checking account you can get around this problem by opening an account that is noninterest bearing. With a savings account some banks will allow you to register the account as owned by a nonprofit group (your reunion committee) even though technically you are not nonprofit. The banks are simply trying to stay on the good side of the federal auditors and such an arrangement will usually appease them as long as there is not a huge sum involved. (See Chapter 12 for information on nonprofit family reunion groups.)

It's best to deal with banks where you or someone in your group is well known. If someone in your family works in a bank, so much the better. Keep in mind that a bank manager *does* have the authority to set up the accounts in the manner described above. If you find yourself dealing with a "new accounts" clerk who seems reluctant, ask to speak with the manager. If that doesn't work, try another bank.

Bookkeeping

The actual business bookkeeping (bank deposits, bank balance, bills due and paid, etc.) should be done on a double-entry spreadsheet. But exact bookkeeping instructions are beyond the scope of this book. If you don't know how to keep double entry books, find someone who does. This is especially important for family associations. If necessary, hire a book-keeper or at the very least, hire a professional to set up the books. This is the most time consuming and technical part, and once it's done, how to continue should be fairly obvious.

Using the Family's Talents
and Resources to Save $$$

Donations, volunteers, and special projects can help re-duce reunion costs. Let members know of your needs and make suggestions about how they can help. Does someone own a printing company that might donate paper or printing? Will a cousin with a large home garden or farm donate fruits or vegetables for meals? Are there children who would lick stamps and put address labels on the envelopes?

Put an "items needed" and "help wanted" list in every mailer along with a request to return it by a certain date. This "check-what-you-can-do" system gets results and allows people to volunteer who otherwise might feel too pressured if asked directly.

You might want to plan a special fund-raising activity before the reunion to cover extra costs. If the family teenagers would like to have music and dancing at the reunion, en-courage them to organize a car wash to raise funds for a disk jockey. Another popular way to raise money is to have a bake sale. Look around your community for the types of activities local groups do to raise money. Fund-raising has an added benefit: Involving people at this stage of planning will result in more interest in the reunion.

Keep a Financial History

It's helpful to keep a financial history. The process for planning a first reunion is the same as for a 20th except that you should have been saving your financial information from year to year for comparison.

Your financial history should list estimated expenses, actual expenses, and the difference between them. After the reunion, review the numbers and jot down thoughts that come to mind. Keep a notebook listing all of your assumptions, considerations, calculations, suggestions, and mistakes. This helps you (or someone else) prepare for future reunions and hopefully eliminate hidden costs and surprises. Take the time to do it right; write it so someone else can make sense of it.

A financial history is absolutely necessary to get the best possible group rates from hotels and resorts—and the larger your group, the more important this is (see "Negotiating and Contracts" in Chapter 1). Hotels and resorts will not give their best rates based on speculation. You must "prove" your past reunion attendance for them to seriously listen to you.

CHAPTER 4

Keeping Records

Keep It Simple – Types of Information – Filing Systems–
Example of a Record Keeping System – Coding / Earmarking –
Lists – Other Important Information – Other Useful Tips –
Using Computers.

Keep It Simple

Regardless of the size of your group, you will need to create
a system to keep information on family members. In this chapter there is more material than you will need on record keeping. Evaluate the possibilities, use the information that
pertains to your situation, and disregard the rest. You should
create the *simplest* system that will give you what you need.
For example, some families are so small they know where
everyone is. Such a group would have no need to record information on finding, re-finding, and tracing people. It would only
need a system to record addresses and financial transactions.

For the sake of clarity, let's discuss some of the terminology in this chapter. *Organizing and updating information* is referred to as "record keeping." A "record" is *the information pertaining to one individual plus his or her immediate family.* A "file" is *a group of records.* A "list" is *accumulated information derived from these files,* usually in printed form.

Types of Information

Two types of information are most useful: "personal" and "financial."

Personal Information. Here is a list of personal information that can be collected for your records:

- Address, phone number (mailing list).
- Biographical information.
- Replies to surveys.
- All information that led to finding a person or family.
- Information that can lead to "re-finding" a person or family.
- Information furnished to help find others.
- Skills, services volunteered, goods donated or available.
- Special dietary or personal needs.
- Financial information (see below).

Financial Information. A financial file on each family should be maintained separately from the business or bookkeeping records. For a one-time reunion (or a first-time reunion), this financial information could simply go on the bottom of the record as in Figure 5E. However, groups that have reunions regularly should have a separate "financial file." This could be a separate card file arranged by last name. Or you could add a "financial card" (use a special color) behind the name card in your regular file. The financial file contains information on all on-going financial transactions such as:

✓ Registration fees paid/owed.

✓ Dues paid/owed.

✓ Donations.

✓ Merchandise bought/ordered.

The information in this file should include check numbers, the dates they were deposited, and the items paid for. This is important because, in most cases, this record of deposit is the only verification available at the reunion.

Filing Systems

There are three ways the files can be kept:

1. On file cards (one name or family per card). 4 x 6 cards are better than 3 x 5s because they hold more information. If more room is needed, add cards behind the first (use a different color for additional cards).

2. In a 3-ring binder (one name or family per sheet of paper). This is the best way (other than using a computer) for reunion groups that intend to put a lot of time and effort into finding extended family members. Some "finds" may take several years and a lot of searching. In such cases, an $8\frac{1}{2}$ x 11 binder system is more efficient than a card system because it will hold more information. Add sheets as necessary.

3. On computer disk. Computers are amazingly efficient and time saving, but to go this route you should have someone with experience or who is willing to put in the time and effort that computers require. See "Using Computers," p. 52.

Example of a Record Keeping System

Records are usually filed by last name—one record per family or per individual if a person has no family. As children leave home or become adults, they are given their own records.

Refer to the flow chart on p. 44. All names that have no address or an "improbable" address, start off in the *"Where RU?" file.* Your intention is to eventually make this file as small as possible. An "improbable" address is an old address that you wouldn't bother wasting a stamp on. You should not discard this address, however; it can still prove useful if you have time to visit the neighbors and ask questions or use the "city directory" method to find them (see p. 168).

Once you have a mailing address, the record goes into the *mailing file* which is divided into verified and unverified addres-

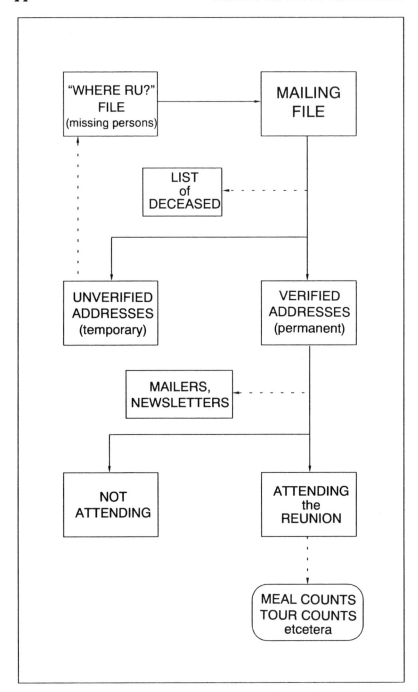

FIGURE 4. A flow chart for the example described on p. 43.

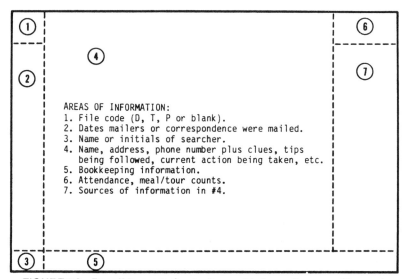

① ⑥

④ ⑦

②

AREAS OF INFORMATION:
1. File code (D, T, P or blank).
2. Dates mailers or correspondence were mailed.
3. Name or initials of searcher.
4. Name, address, phone number plus clues, tips
   being followed, current action being taken, etc.
5. Bookkeeping information.
6. Attendance, meal/tour counts.
7. Sources of information in #4.

③ ⑤

FIGURE 5A. Possible areas for codes and information on a file card.

PHYLLIS JONES

- MOVED TO PORTLAND, ORE. OUT OF ⟩ NELLIE (209) 555-1234
  HIGH SCHOOL.
- MARRIED A SCHOOLMATE SENIOR YEAR ⟩ UNCLE AL (503) 555-3456
  AT SMITH COLLEGE
4-15 - SENT LETTER TO SMITH COLLEGE ALUMNI
       ASSN, TO BE FORWARDED

PAM

FIGURE 5B. First of all, the card itself is of a certain color designating a
particular branch of the family. Information is accumulated gradually.
Two people (names on right) recall that she moved to Portland to go to
school and that she married while in college. A letter to be forwarded to
her (see p. 164) was sent to the alumni association of the school. The
searcher's name is in the lower left corner.

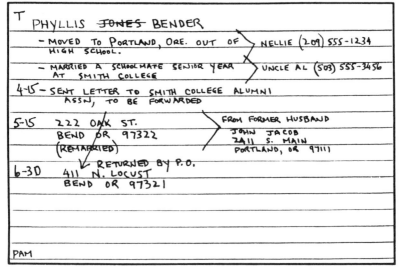

T
PHYLLIS ~~JONES~~ BENDER

- MOVED TO PORTLAND, ORE. OUT OF   > NELLIE (209) 555-1234
  HIGH SCHOOL.

- MARRIED A SCHOOLMATE SENIOR YEAR   > UNCLE AL (503) 555-3456
  AT SMITH COLLEGE

4-15 - SENT LETTER TO SMITH COLLEGE ALUMNI
      ASSN, TO BE FORWARDED

5-15   222 OAK ST.   FROM FORMER HUSBAND
       BEND OR 97322   JOHN JACOB
       (REMARRIED)   2411 S. MAIN
                                      PORTLAND, OR 97111

PAM

FIGURE 5C. *Phyllis' former husband received the letter and sent along an address. She is now remarried. All names are recorded. A mailer is sent to this address on 5-15. A "T" (for Temporary address) is put in the upper left corner.*

T
PHYLLIS ~~JONES~~ BENDER

- MOVED TO PORTLAND, ORE. OUT OF   > NELLIE (209) 555-1234
  HIGH SCHOOL.

- MARRIED A SCHOOLMATE SENIOR YEAR   > UNCLE AL (503) 555-3456
  AT SMITH COLLEGE

4-15 - SENT LETTER TO SMITH COLLEGE ALUMNI
      ASSN, TO BE FORWARDED

5-15   222 OAK ST.   FROM FORMER HUSBAND
       BEND OR 97322   JOHN JACOB
       (REMARRIED)   2411 S. MAIN
                                      PORTLAND, OR 97111
             RETURNED BY P.O.
6-30   411 N. LOCUST
       BEND OR 97321

PAM

FIGURE 5D. *The address furnished by her former husband turns out to be old, but because "Address Correction Requested" was written on the envelope, the Post Office returned the mailer with the updated address. The mailer was then sent to the new address on 6-31.*

```
┌─────────────────────────────────────────────────────────────────┐
│ ᴾ                                                          ④      │
│   PHYLLIS  J̶O̶N̶E̶S̶  BENDER                                        │
│    ─ MOVED TO PORTLAND, ORE. OUT OF      NELLIE (209) 555-1234    │
│      HIGH SCHOOL.                                                 │
│    ─ MARRIED A SCHOOLMATE SENIOR YEAR    UNCLE AL (503) 555-3456  │
│      AT  SMITH COLLEGE                                            │
│  4-15 ─ SENT LETTER TO SMITH COLLEGE ALUMNI                      │
│        ASSN, TO BE FORWARDED                                      │
│  5-15   222 OAK ST.              FROM FORMER HUSBAND             │
│         BEND OR 97322            JOHN  JACOB                      │
│         (REMARRIED)              2411 S. MAIN                     │
│                                  PORTLAND, OR  97111             │
│  6-30  ┌─ RETURNED BY P.O.                                       │
│        │ 411 N. LOCUST                                           │
│        │ BEND OR 97321  │(503) 555-2424                          │
│                                                                  │
│                                                        OVER →    │
│ ─────────────────────────────────────────────────────────────  │
│ PAM│ PAID FOR: 2 ADULTS  $20, #263 7-15                         │
│              2 KIDS                                              │
└─────────────────────────────────────────────────────────────────┘
```

FIGURE 5E. **Phyllis responds and sends the $20 fee for herself, her husband, and two children. A box is drawn around her verified address and the T is changed to a P (for Permanent address). The date of deposit and check number are recorded on the bottom of the card, and a circled "4" in the upper right corner indicates that 4 people from her family will be attending.**

```
┌─────────────────────────────────────────────────────────────────┐
│   HUSBAND :  RALPH                                               │
│   OCCUPATION :  ELECTRICIAN                                      │
│   HER OCCUPATION :  PART-TIME CLERK                              │
│   CHILDREN :  KIM 14, ALICE 12                                   │
│   HOBBIES :  CAMPING                                             │
│                                                                  │
│   ─ PHONED 7-2                                                   │
│   ─ WILL HELP WITH REGISTRATION                                  │
│   ─ WILL BRING HER GRANDMOTHER'S DIARY                          │
│   ─ SAYS HER COUSIN MARGIE JONES IS                             │
│     MARRIED AND LIVING IN NEWPORT, RI.                          │
│     WILL TRY TO GET HER ADDRESS.                                │
│                                                                  │
└─────────────────────────────────────────────────────────────────┘
```

FIGURE 5F. **(Back of card) On 7-2 she calls to offer her help with registration and has some information about her cousin, Margie Jones. The biographical information came from a survey sent with the mailer.**

ses. The verified addresses can further be divided into those attending the reunion and those not attending. The important thing to remember is these *sub-files* do not necessarily have to be physically separated from each other as long as they are marked or coded so that you can easily tell the status of each record at a glance (see "Coding/Earmarking," below).

On the other hand, if your group is small and/or you have a good memory, you might want to separate out some sub-files. The problem with separating the files comes when you want to check on the status of a particular family or individual and you can't remember exactly where the record is. With separated files, in order to find the record, you may have to go through all the files. The general rules are:

✓ The fewer the sub-files (that are physically separated from each other), the easier it will be to find a particular record.

✓ The larger the group, the more you should try to keep your files consolidated.

See "status list," below, for a tip on how to maintain large separated files.

All records in the mailing file have addresses you intend to mail to; therefore, the mailing labels are derived directly from this file. Remember, there are two types of addresses in this file, verified and unverified. An address is unverified until you know for sure that it is accurate. (Just because a mailer doesn't come back by return mail, doesn't necessarily mean the addressee received it.) Unverified addresses plus the "Where RU?" file make up the missing person list.

Coding/Earmarking

Coding means marking a record or list by writing on it. Colored ink or pencil can be used for indicating different categories of information. For example, use red ink for bookkeeping information and green for mailing information. The "position" of the code can be informative, too (see Figure 5A).

The upper left corner of a card can contain a code indicating which sub-file the record is in. No code (blank) means the record is still in the "Where RU?" file. A "D" indicates a deceased person; a "T" (for Temporary) is used for an unverified address ; a "P" (for Permanent) is a verified address. Note that a T easily becomes a P without having to erase. A box is drawn around a verified address (use colored ink).

The mailing date in the left side margin indicates when a mailing was sent, and appears next to the address that the mailer was sent to. If two mailers are sent, both dates should be recorded. If a "lost" person is "found" just before the reunion, and, as a result, both mailers are sent together, the date is underlined twice.

The bottom left corner contains the searcher's initials. This way you always know who is (or was) in charge of finding the person. If a different searcher is assigned, put the new searcher's initials above the first.

Earmarking is a way of marking a record without writing on it. It can be done with paper clips or colored self-stick dots. There are also plastic clips made for file cards called "file card signals." These work somewhat like a paper clip, but stick up above the card. A similar item are Post-It Tape Flags that come in bright colors, can be written on, and are removable. (For sources, see the Appendix, Dot Paste-Up Supply.)

The position of the marker on the card could also have a meaning. For example, a paper clip on the left top of a card could mean one thing and on the right top could mean another. The same goes for color coding. Most clips, including the metal ones, are available in colors. Possible reasons for earmarking: owes money, paid for family photo but can't attend, volunteered to work during reunion, candidate for an award, has special presentation or skit for the program, etc.

Both coding and earmarking save a lot of time; however, you must figure out *beforehand* what they are going to mean. Making up meanings as you go along can create confusion. Keep a list of the meanings of your codes to remind yourself and others who might inherit or use the files.

Lists

As mentioned before, a "list" is accumulated information that is derived from these files, usually in printed form. For example:

- Missing person or missing family list (a printout of the "Where RU?" file).
- Those attending the reunion.
- Those not yet arrived.
- Meal counts, tour counts, etc.
- Survey and statistical information.
- Those owing money.
- Award candidates.
- Those who volunteered for jobs.
- Deceased list.

If you have a large group (and, therefore, large files), a *status list* can be useful because it allows you to keep your files separated and still be able to quickly find the status of a particular record. The status list is simply a list of your group in alphabetical order. Next to each name put the file code (see previous page).

It is often helpful if a list and its corresponding records are linked by a note, code or earmark. For example, as you add a name to the list of people attending the reunion, be sure a code appears on that person's record. In this case, a circled number in the upper right hand corner would do. The number within the circle indicates the number of people attending from that family (adding these numbers from all cards gives you the attendance count). Then if the attendance list is lost, it can easily be re-created by checking all records for a circled number in the upper right corner.

You could put other coded information in this list, thereby eliminating the need to create other lists. For example, "$X" means "owes money" (write it in red); "$GP" means "can't attend, but paid for group photo"; etc. Again, always be sure an equivalent code or earmark appears on the individual records so if the list is lost, it can be re-created.

Other Important Information

Other categories of information that can be contained in, or derived from these files are:

1. Information for tracing people. When you collect information, write down everything: sources talked to, databases checked, letters written, dead-ends followed, phone calls made, etc. Date each entry. You are leaving a "trace"—a running record or log of all the steps taken to find a person. If someone else takes over the search, they won't have to reinvent the wheel. Also, if the person disappears again, a "re-find" will be much easier, and dead-ends can be avoided.

Some family organizations intentionally collect information for the purpose of more easily "re-finding" a person. Social security number, driver's license number, service number, birthdate, and next of kin (or "someone who will always know where you are") all fall under this category.

2. Clues for finding people. Indicate on the back of each record any names, tips, or other information that a person has provided for finding other people. Sometimes it's handy to know the source of information in order to know who to contact for more leads or to verify the original information.

3. Biographical information. If using cards to collect data, put this information on the back or on a separate card (different color) filed behind the first. The amount of biographical information you collect can vary (see "The Survey," p. 64). Names and birthdates are minimum family data to record. File cards are limited in the amount of information they can hold, therefore, more information should be kept in a separate file, such as a 3-ring binder.

4. Helpful notes on each family. Keep notes about each family, such as services and donations they have offered, skills they have that may come in handy, items that could be borrowed, homes available for accommodations, special transportation needed for elderly and/or handicapped, special requests, dietary needs, etc.

5. Missing Person List ("Where RU?" file). If it's not too long, this list should be updated and sent out with each mailing or newsletter.

Other Useful Tips

✓ *The less you copy and recopy information, the better.* Stick with the original record; cross out the old info and add the new. *Don't erase*—the old information may prove useful if all other leads die out. (Old information is especially useful to future reunions because if a family member "disappears" again, the old sources will be the most likely to help relocate the person.) If the front and back of the card become full, add a second card behind the first, paper clipping the two cards together.

✓ *Be sure to save all information.* It's best if one person is in charge of the records, preferably someone who will not be changing addresses often. Give copies of the address and phone number list to two or three other people for safekeeping. Announce who is in charge of the address list in your mailings and at the reunion so that people can send change-of-address announcements to that person. Also, have copies of the address list available at the reunion along with scratch paper so people can copy the addresses of family members they would like to stay in touch with. A profitable alternative is to offer a family directory for sale (see Chapter 10).

✓ As your file grows and contains more and more information (especially financial information), it becomes more valuable. Take good care of it. Don't loan it—not even a portion of it. All of the information, even just a name, is valuable. If someone wants to try their luck at finding some people, don't give them the records, not even the ones that contain names only. Give them a list of the names instead or a separate copied group of records, but never the original set. If your information is on computer disks or hard drive, insist that the operator maintain a back-up copy.

✓ Address labels, file card trays (metal or plastic and in three sizes), and file cards (lined, plain, and in colors), 3-ring binders and paper are available from Quill Corporation and others. See the Appendix.

Using Computers

Most reunion records are kept on file cards or in 3-ring binders. However, the personal computer is changing these somewhat time consuming methods. If you have access to a home computer with a printer, by all means use it. However, unless you have time to experiment, this may not be the best option. Be sure the operator has "hands on" experience with both the computer and the software. If you are converting your system to computer, maintain parallel paper files until you are sure the computer system is working properly. And always have a "back up" system to protect your information.

A computer can streamline the whole process of creating, updating, and maintaining your filing system. You will be able to insert each new address alphabetically with a keystroke. Biographical information, a missing person list, a list of those attending the reunion, printed address labels, or a meal count can be run off at any time. You are only limited by the software and the experience and ability of the operator. With the sophisticated personal computers and software of today, the ability to program is not a necessary skill.

(For information on electronic bulletin boards and commercial computer networks, see p. 166. For information on desktop publishing, see p. 185.)

CHAPTER 5

Family Communication:
Mailers/Newsletters/Surveys

Mailers: Announcing the Reunion – Contents of the Mailer – Who Gets the Mailers? – A Family Newsletter– Round Robin Letters– The Family Survey.

The term "mailer," as used in this book, refers to the notices sent to announce a particular reunion. A newsletter, on the other hand, serves as a small family newspaper and is published periodically.

Mailers: Announcing the Reunion

The main link between your family members and the reunion is through the mail. Most of the impressions, ideas, and opinions—good, bad, or indifferent—that will be formed about the upcoming reunion, will come from the printed material that is sent out. It will be read and scrutinized very carefully, and may carry much more weight and import than you realize. The observation that reunion notices get casually tossed into the trash like junk mail is a myth. If they end up in the trash, it's only after serious consideration. Even then, they may be fished out again.

Mailers that are carelessly worded, have missing or incorrect information, or appear sloppy convey the impression that the reunion will turn out the same way, and give the reader a good excuse to say, "no thanks." We assure you that the time spent to produce high quality, thoughtfully worded mailers is worth your effort. They will not only help your reunion succeed socially by encouraging greater attendance, but economically as well. This is because greater attendance means more people to share the costs, and, therefore, less cost per person.

If your reunion is small and local, your mailer can simply contain "what, where, when, what to bring, and how to get there":

```
What:   Davis Family Reunion
When:   As usual, the second Saturday in August:
        This year, August 10th.
Where:  At Aunt Anna's and Uncle Jake's, 10499
        Reed Avenue, (209) 555-2944.
Time:   2 p.m. to 9 p.m.
Bring:  Potluck dish of your choice and drinks for
        five people, photographs of your family
        from the past year. Eating utensils will
        be provided.
Take:   Route 12 to intersection of Maple, turn
        left, go 2 lights to Oak, turn right, 3rd
        house (red brick) on left. See you there!
```

Mailers can be simple invitations (as above) or more elaborate announcements. If you have family members who are good with words or talented at graphics, engage them in helping with the mailers. A family member may even have a publishing program to try out on their computer.

FIGURE 6. *An example of a family reunion invitation from the 1890's.*

If you make the mailer fun and interesting, it will set a similar tone for your whole reunion. Figures 7A and 7B show the difference between a regular reunion mailer and one that uses a more interesting format. *The wording in each is exactly the same and the same typewriter was used.* The fancier format is really not that hard to do. The necessary techniques, terms, and resources are explained in Chapter 14.

Contents of the Mailers:

Essential:

✓ date, time and location of the reunion.

✓ return address and phone number.

✓ registration fees/registration form.

✓ payment procedure.

✓ cancellation policy and refunding rules.

✓ how to get there (general driving instructions)

Optional:

✓ list of committee members with phone numbers.

✓ short history of decisions made and those in progress.

✓ ask for comments and suggestions; ideas for the program; award categories and prizes; volunteers; information on "missing" family members; memorabilia such as old photos, movies, videos, scrapbooks, Bibles, photo albums, old letters, family trees, genealogies, newspaper clippings, etc.

✓ advance registration incentives.

✓ a survey.

✓ give name, address, and phone number of person in charge of mailing list.

✓ names and phone numbers of places and people with available accommodations, such as family members, bed and breakfasts, hotels, motels, and RV campsites in the area.

✓ give approximate date of the next mailer.

✓ include jokes, cartoons, interesting trivia, and historical data.

The last mailer before the reunion could include:

✓ updated information, last minute news, changes, or additions to original plans.

✓ encouragement for borderliners and procrastinators. (A list of those planning to attend will often entice others.)

✓ a reunion schedule or description of program/events.

✓ a hand-drawn or simplified map showing family homes, reunion location, airport(s), train station(s), and main highways.

✓ driving instructions to the reunion location.

✓ phone numbers of car rental agencies.

✓ bus, taxi, or limo prices.

✓ type of weather to expect.

✓ what to wear.

✓ another reminder to bring old photos and memorabilia, to wear family T-shirts, buttons, etc.

Note: There may be other items to include in the mailers which will pertain specifically to your reunion, such as food and sports equipment to bring.

Frequency. One mailer is not enough; two is better; three is best. We recommend three for each reunion because it's more effective in getting a diverse and scattered group of people to respond. The first should come out 9–12 months before the reunion, the second 4–6 months before, and the last 4–6 weeks before.

Who Gets the Mailers?

Send the first mailer to everyone on your address list. If you have a large family and at first lack addresses, send mailers to family heads asking them to duplicate them and pass them on to their children and grandchildren. Or make it easy for them—send copies they can mail on. If the family elders cannot carry out this task, pick one of their children who can do it for them. Be sure to pick those known for their ability to "follow through" and who have the time and interest.

January 19xx

Dear Family:

Thanks to Aunt Lou's efforts, it looks like there's enough interest in a family reunion to go ahead and schedule one. You may recall that she sent out a survey last Fall asking us if we'd like to have a reunion. She's also made a LOT of phone calls since then, and the consensus is that this summer is a good time for our first family reunion in over 30 years. Over 60 people have signed up.

So we rented the pavilion in Roeding Park in Fresno for August 18 and 19 (Saturday and Sunday). There's lots of shade, room for the kids to play, BBQ grills, tables, softball field, and a zoo next door. The petting zoo is available Sunday PM.

In order to pay our expenses, we've decided to charge $15 per household to attend the reunion. This covers mailing, phone calls and deposits. We need your money the sooner the better. Please don't wait until the reunion to pay. Make checks out to: Carson Family Reunion.

FOOD. There will be a catered BBQ Sunday noon. This will cost $7 per adult and $4 for kids under 12. The meal Saturday night will be potluck, which I will coordinate by phone. Lisa (209) 555-4444.

FIGURE 7A. This is a portion of a typical reunion mailer. Now see Figure 7B.

𝕽𝖊𝖚𝖓𝖎𝖔𝖓 𝕹𝖊𝖜𝖘

SPECIAL REUNION EDITION
January, 19xx

LET'S GET
TOGETHER
Aug. 18-19

Thanks to Aunt Lou's efforts, it looks like there's enough interest in a family reunion to go ahead and schedule one. You may recall that she sent out a survey last Fall asking us if we'd like to have a reunion. She's also made a LOT of phone calls since then, and the consensus is that this summer is a good time for our first family reunion in over 30 years. Over 60 people have signed up.

So we rented the pavilion in Roeding Park in Fresno for Aug. 18-19 (Sat & Sun). There's lots of shade, room for the kids to play, BBQ grills, tables, softball field, and a zoo next door. The petting zoo is available Sunday PM.

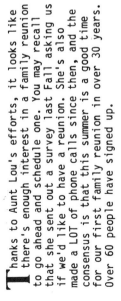 IF YOU HAVE ANY QUESTIONS ABOUT THE REUNION, CALL OR WRITE: Lisa Carson Smith, 1234 Eucalyptus St., Fresno, CA 92711, (209) 555-4444.

HELP!

IN ORDER TO PAY OUR EXPENSES, we've decided to charge $15 per household to attend the reunion. This covers mailing, phone calls and deposits. We need your money the sooner the better. Please don't wait until the reunion to pay. Make checks out to: "Carson Family Reunion" and send to our treasurer: Lou Carson, 123 Oak St., Albany, NY 13456.

    *   *   *   *   *   *   *

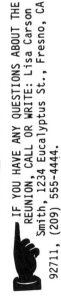 FOOD. There will be a catered BBQ Sunday noon. This will cost $7 per-adult and $4 for kids under 12. To attend this meal, fill out the enclosed form. The meal Saturday night will be potluck, which I will coordinate by phone. Lisa: (209) 555-4444.

FIGURE 7B. This is the same mailer as Figure 7A, but put into a newsletter format. The same typewriter and exactly the same wording was used in both. The difference is some clip art, some transfer lettering, and a photocopy reduction.

If your family lived in a closely-knit, friendly neighborhood, you might want to invite some of the neighbors. Also, consider inviting the minister of your church, favorite teachers and principals from the schools, the family doctor, or a mail carrier. One family invited the nanny their children had when they were small. Anyone who "feels like family" would be a good addition to your group.

A Family Newsletter

A newsletter is like a family newspaper. It becomes a "thread" that ties people together and keeps them interested in the "goings-on" of the family, including reunions, over a long period of time. A newsletter is an excellent forum to campaign for, discuss, and announce a family reunion.

However, newsletters can be time consuming, and the decision to start one should ultimately rest with one person willing to do the work—the editor. No matter how simple the publication, there are basic tasks that must be done. Information must be gathered. It must be typed in some format, printed, collated, folded, addressed, stamped, and mailed. The fancier ones require some graphic and design ability, unless you have that aspect hired out. The larger the mailing list and the larger the newsletter, the more time consuming the project.

The second consideration is the cost. Printing and mailing will be your biggest expense. Most families charge a yearly subscription fee. If you want all the family members to receive the newsletter, but not everyone is willing to subscribe, you must have a plan to absorb the costs or raise money to cover them. Annual subscriptions to family newsletters generally range from $2 to $15 and vary from one to four issues.

Getting started. So you've just been appointed editor of your family's newsletter. You know what a typewriter is, how to look up words in a dictionary, and that's about it. What to do?

First, get samples of other newsletters. Each year the *Genealogical Helper* (see address in the Appendix) prints a list of family newsletters. Write to some of these asking for samples. Be sure to include a donation to cover the issue cost and postage. (The *Genealogical Helper* will add your family newsletter to its yearly list if you send them a copy.)

Next, choose a name for your newsletter. The editor can choose it or the family can have a contest, voting on the final choice with a prize of a free subscription for the winner. Names for newsletters range from the sedate—Thomas Sloan Markay Association Bulletin—to something lighter, such as Chapman Chatter, Butcher's Block, Bell's Chime, or Grin and Barrett. Most names, however, tell it as it is—Stone Newsletter, Schneider News, Hay's Paper.

The next step is to develop a letterhead and format for your newsletter. This can be hired out to professionals or you can study some graphic techniques and design and do your own. Turn to Chapter 14 for information on these subjects.

The simplest newsletter consists of accumulated letters from family members. These are collected, photocopied as is, stapled together, and mailed out to everyone who contributed a letter or to everyone on your mailing list. The front page could have a special letterhead plus news and information from the editor. If you create this type of newsletter and mail it in early December, it can replace exchanging holiday cards and letters among family members. Or you can mail it in November with a complete address list so families can use it when sending their greeting cards. Yet another approach is to mail it mid-year so that the family receives correspondence at a time when it normally doesn't. (Also see "Round Robin Letters," next page.)

It doesn't take too much extra effort to make a newsletter entertaining. It could contain recipes, articles about family events, photos, a column, quizzes and puzzles, trivia, clip-art, cartoons, birthdays, jokes, etc. Such a friendly approach generates interest and allows the newsletter to become a vehicle for creating stronger family bonds. (See "Include Some Entertainment," in Chapter 14.)

You can gather material from various families in the form of letters, articles, or responses to a questionnaire. A questionnaire can ask about recent family events: births, graduations, awards, promotions, achievements, deaths, illnesses, travel, moves, marriages, etc. Ask for photographs, old newspaper clippings, children's art work, poems or stories—anything that would convey interesting information about your family.

You may want to write more formal articles in the style of an editorial, a column, or biographical sketches on relatives living or deceased. New findings in genealogy charts or records might be included.

Frequency. The frequency of a newsletter is usually dependent upon the free time of the editor. One to four times per year is common, but we've seen extremes from one every two years to monthly. Another possibility is to publish an "occasion-al"—this means it comes out whenever the editor feels like it. If it comes out less than three times per year, *and* you are planning a reunion, send an additional flyer or two to remind people of the reunion. Subscriptions to an "occasional" newsletter should be based per issue. For example: $15 per 4 issues rather than $15 per year.

Round Robin Letters

The simplest type of family communication with the lowest cost is the round robin letter. It works this way: You write a letter telling about your family, then write out a list of names and addresses of relatives that have agreed ahead of time to participate. Send your letter, the mailing list, and a short letter of instructions to the person on the top of the list. A good number of participants is 10 or 15. Each person adds their letter and sends them all on to the next person on the list. When it comes back to you, you remove your first letter, put in a new one, and send it around again.

Round robins can be great fun and a joy to receive. They cut down on your correspondence because you write one letter to many people. They also allow you to be in contact with a greater number of family members. The only cost is your postage each time you send it on. But round robins are successful only if the participants are willing to keep the letter moving. Some families have a rule that you add your letter within two weeks or send it on without your contribution.

The Family Survey

A survey of your family can provide interesting information. However, there is no use going to the extra trouble unless you know for sure that you will compile and use the results. Here are some ways that a survey can be used:

1. *To provide information for awards to be presented during the reunion program.* Decide on the award categories first, then formulate the questions that will provide the answers. Or it may be more appropriate to ask for the following type of response: "If any of you think you may qualify, or you can suggest someone else who qualifies for any of these awards, please let us know: Most Recent Parent/Grandparent, First to Retire, Youngest Great Grandparent, Traveled the Farthest." Of course, you should still not judge the winner solely by the responses received. Some people will not bother to send back the survey or feel too modest to do so. Just before each winner is announced at the program, ask if anyone can better the record in question. See p. 90 for of more award categories and suggestions.

2. *To compile biographical information for a family directory, a newsletter, a genealogy, or a family history.* The minimal information to gather: name, address, phone number, spouse's name, and children's names. The next level of detail to gather could include occupation(s), birth and marriage dates, and hobbies. Beyond that you might request a short biography of a family; a favorite quote, saying, or proverb; favorite books, movies, or music; and pet peeve.

3. (For large groups) *To collect information that can be used later to "re-find" a person who gets "lost."* Ask for birthdate, social security number, military service number, driver's license number, or address of "someone who will always know where you are." When gathering this type of information, explain your purpose.

4. *To create a chart of "Family Statistics" to be displayed at the reunion.* The chart can also be a part of a directory, a family history, or included in a newsletter. This statistical "family portrait" can include the following:

✓ Total number on mailing list.

✓ Total number present at the reunion.

✓ List of those who live outside of U.S. and/or Canada.

✓ Total number of states represented by group.

✓ List of first-timers attending the reunion.

✓ List of those born, married, died since last reunion.

✓ List of those who have not missed a reunion.

Encourage everyone to fill out and return the survey, even if they can't attend the reunion. Be sure to have survey forms at the registration desk for those who did not send them in.

CHAPTER 6

Mailing: Labels and Postage

Mailing/Postage – Mailing Label Systems – Return Address/ Rubber Stamps.

Mailing/Postage

Each of your mailers or newsletters will probably weigh less than three ounces. Since third class costs the same as first class mail up to that weight (except with a bulk permit), plan on mailing everything first class. First class mail is automatically forwarded (more than once, if necessary), and arrives much more quickly than third class.

Unless you do a large number of mailings per year, we don't recommend a bulk mailing permit (third class mail) because it costs $150 (1992) just to get the permit—$75 per year plus $75 to register. Also your mailers may not be delivered for up to three to four weeks after you mail them. They are last priority for delivery.

Third class bulk mail also requires that you sort the batch by zip code, bundle it, put special stickers on each bundle, weigh them, fill out special forms, and deliver them to the post office (and only the post office that issued the permit). Taking into account the permit cost, preparation time, and possible slow delivery time, it seems wiser to stick with first class mail. Another advantage of first class is that it is automatically returned if it can't be delivered. Third class won't be; it is discarded. However, you can stamp "Address Correction Requested" on the front of third class mail. Then if a forwarding order is on file for the address, the piece of mail will be returned to you with the new address. You pay additional postage on each piece that is returned to you in this way (29¢ for under 1 ounce, 1992) and then you must remail it to the new address.

To mail your newsletters, you can use envelopes or simply fold in thirds or in half, and staple or tape them shut (also see p. 70, "Return Address"). The maximum size for first class mail is 6 $\frac{1}{8}$" x 11 $\frac{1}{2}$" after it's folded. If the piece is folded, it must be stapled or taped shut to qualify as first class mail.

When sending mail to a person in the military overseas, regular domestic rates apply if you use an A.P.O. or F.P.O. address.

Mailing Label Systems

With small families (under 50), addressing envelopes by hand is not a big problem. Of course, a computer that can generate mailing labels makes it very simple. But if you have a large group and no computer, you should plan on some sort of address label system. There are basically two (noncomputer) systems:

1. Peel-off, self-sticking mailing labels come in sheets of 33 (three across the top and 11 down). These sheets are the same size as a sheet of typing paper (8 $\frac{1}{2}$ x 11). You photocopy your list onto these sheets (you may have to take your own labels to the copy shop). To prepare your list, write or type each new address onto a plain white sheet of paper using a label template (see explanation below). Each label entry can be "generally" alphabetized by assigning a certain letter or letters to each sheet. Depending on the size of your group, you may have (for example) the A's, B's, and C's on one sheet, or perhaps just the A's, or you could assign one letter per row of 11 down. The names within each section do not necessarily have to be in alphabetical order. Just before each general mailing, the originals are photocopied onto mailing labels which are then peeled off and stuck onto the mailers.

Another use for these labels, by the way, is to paste one with a new address over the old address on the file cards. If it turns out that the old information becomes of interest again, the label peels off easily (if you use the ones with nonpermanent adhesive). Also, if you want to start a separate financial file system, you could stick the labels onto cards and alphabetize them.

A *label template* comes with each package of labels you buy. It is a regular size sheet of paper with heavy black lines representing the label edges. When placed behind an ordinary sheet of white paper, the black lines show through to guide the placement of the addressing information onto the plain paper (you can type or write). The template is never written or typed on, itself; it functions only as a guide.

2. The second method, which also makes use of self-sticking, peel-off labels, is a commercial system called CopyMaster. (It's available at large office supply or stationery stores, or see the Appendix, Quill Corp.) CopyMaster consists of clear plastic pages ($8\frac{1}{2}$ x 11) with 33 pockets, and cards to insert into these pockets. The plastic pages (which are hole-punched for a 3-ring binder) and insert cards can be bought separately or in a package along with a binder and some address labels. The upper portion of the cards is for mailing information and is the size of a mailing label. The lower portion, which is approximately the same size, is for any other information (see Figure 8). When the cards reside in their pockets, the lower portion doesn't show because the cards overlap each other. This allows you to easily photocopy them onto address labels. The best part of this system is that the

RICHARD STONE
1055 Heaven Street
Cary, NC 27511

Betty   919/467-
2 boys   dob 1
golf   S857
March 76   Art W.

FIGURE 8

file can always be kept in exact alphabetical order because the cards can be moved around as you add new ones (though it takes some time to do so).

Don't bother creating labels for people who are not "found" until just before the reunion—simply hand-address their mailers. If these people missed previous mailings, send them all the prior mailings along with the current one; be sure to enclose a note of explanation to avoid confusion.

If a previous reunion group has left you with no file cards, only a batch of mailing labels or label originals (created using a template), you can create a new card file by photocopying onto new labels, sticking these labels onto cards, and alphabetizing the cards.

When photocopying onto labels, be sure to use a machine that copies at 100% (same size as original). Many machines slightly magnify (around 102–103%) the original as it is copied. This can cause the copy to spill over the boundaries of the label, and you may end up with partial information on some labels (see Figure 9). This happens especially when making copies of copies. The newer machines have the option of copying at 100%, but you may have to ask for it.

Return Address/Rubber Stamps

If you are folding your mailer or newsletter in thirds for mailing instead of using envelopes, you can have the return address printed in the upper left corner of the "mailing face" (the appropriate third of your outside sheet) and "First Class Mail" and "Address Correction Requested" printed in the bottom left corner. Be sure to include a phone number along with the return address. If you don't print the return address on the mailer, you can order pre-printed return address labels that are self-stick and peel-off. A third option is to invest in a few rubber stamps.

Possibilities for rubber stamps:

1. Return address (include phone number).
2. "(family name) FAMILY REUNION INFORMATION ENCLOSED"
3. "ADDRESS CORRECTION REQUESTED" (see p. 68).
4. "FIRST CLASS MAIL"
5. Family crest.

Ordered through office supply stores, these stamps can all be used with brightly colored inks for emphasis and decorative effect. There are printers or office supply stores in larger towns and cities where you can get rubber stamps the same day you place the order.

Pre-printed return address labels (gummed or self-stick) are available very cheaply from Walter Drake and Sons (see the Appendix). They may take four to eight weeks for delivery. Order early.

Number 10 (long) envelopes with your return address printed in the upper left hand corner (minimum order is 1000) are available from Quill Corp. (see the Appendix). Imprinted envelopes also come in quantities of 100 from Walter Drake and Sons.

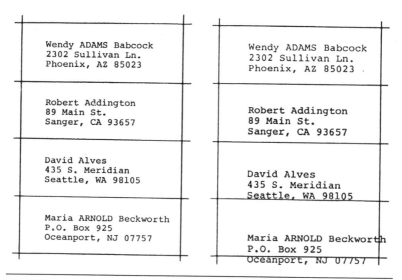

FIGURE 9. *Because some photocopy machines slightly magnify the image, making copies of copies can result in addresses over-spilling their bounds. Always copy from the original or at 100%.*

CHAPTER 7

Getting Ready:
Services, Supplies, and Special Touches

Help from the Commercial Community – Being Good Hosts –
Registration – Family Identification – Name Tags – Decorations –
Music – Activities – The Program – In Memoriam – Planning for
Emergencies – Tipping.

Help from the Commercial Community

As plans for your reunion progress, needs will develop for
certain services and supplies. Before you purchase anything or
go looking elsewhere, find out what is offered by the Convention Bureau and Chamber of Commerce in the area where your
reunion will be held. Their services and supplies vary widely,
but they all offer something. Some things may be provided
free; for others there may be a nominal charge. The larger your
reunion, the more value it is to the commercial community,
and the more help you can get.

Below is a list of possible services and supplies that may be available. Most Convention Bureaus and Chambers of Commerce offer no more than two or three of these. Some may be available from convention centers and hotels as well.

✓ Help with site inspection.

✓ Discounts with airlines.

✓ Name tags, badges, banners, table decorations, signs.

✓ Gifts of local merchandise.

✓ "Shells" (One-page flyers containing local information or ads with space for your reunion program. Printing is usually provided free.)

✓ Maps, local information brochures, official greeting/welcome letter from the mayor, and other give-aways to include in your registration packets.

✓ Cash boxes.

✓ Copy machines/typewriters to use during registration.

✓ Photocopying and printing services.

✓ Parking permits.

✓ Registration cards.

✓ Mailing services.

✓ Secretarial services.

✓ Shopping programs.

✓ Sightseeing trips.

✓ Phone books.

Being Good Hosts

Hospitality can make the difference between a good reunion and a really great one. Often it's the little things that make you and your committee members gracious hosts. Here are some examples:

✓ Have "greeters" at the front door pointing the way to the registration area and answering any questions.

✓ Have enough people staffing the registration table during "rush hour."

✓ At large reunions, identify the main staff and "people who can answer questions" with special hats, caps, or badges.

✓ Give first-timers special attention. Make it easy for them to mix.

✓ Give recognition to old-timers with awards, special name tags, etc.

✓ Reach out. Help the person who appears lost.

✓ Provide local gifts (e.g., salt water taffy in Atlantic City, maple syrup in Vermont).

✓ Serve refreshments and/or play music during registration.

✓ Use glasses instead of plastic cups.

✓ Put flowers in the rooms of honored guests.

✓ Decorate with flowers.

✓ Provide free or validated parking.

Such thoughtful yet inexpensive considerations will help make this reunion a hit, and will go a long way toward making the next reunion a success as well. When you've made the people feel comfortable, they are more likely to have a good time and will want to attend the next reunion.

Get Ready for Registration

The registration area is the "front door" to your reunion, and its atmosphere and organization will set the tone for the remainder of the event. First impressions are lasting impressions. It's important to have an efficient, painless, practical registration at your reunion.

✓ Carefully think through the whole process of registration: forms, kits, tickets, name tags, varification, receipts, refunds, etc. Try to anticipate and solve problems that may arise.

✓ The registration area should be easy to locate, with signs pointing the way. This is especially true if another activity is taking place simultaneously (as often happens in convention centers and large hotels).

✓ Make sure supplies and furniture are ordered well in advance. Items might include tables, chairs, wastebaskets, signs, typewriter, paper, cash boxes, change, marking pens, scotch tape, masking tape, paper clips, scissors, staplers, pens, pencils, etc.

✓ Greeters should be stationed at the entrance area in front of the registration table. Their job is to make everyone feel welcome and comfortable, and to answer questions. Remind them to stay focused on their job and not drift away into private conversations.

✓ Develop a registration "kit" or "packet." This is simply a manila envelope full of everything the person or family will need for the event. It can contain local information, tour information, maps, local give-aways, name tags, event tickets, the reunion program, a survey, evaluation questionnaire, family directory, etc. These packets are "stuffed" ahead of time and each envelope has the family's or individual's name on the outside, printed in big letters. For large reunions, arrange them in alphabetical order.

✓ Provide a list of those who have paid and those who owe money. Keep all financial records at the registration table. Each family's financial standing can be written on, or stapled to, the packet.

✓ Provide relief for greeters and those doing the registering. No volunteer should do this for more than an hour without a break. If the person is being paid (such as hotel staff), they should still be relieved occasionally.

Family Identification

It may happen that some family members will first set eyes on each other at the registration desk. Which Brown are you related to? Is Paul or Earl your father? Keeping clans straight can be facilitated by some visual helpers prepared ahead of time.

Families around the country have come up with clever systems of dressing that make family identification easier at the reunion. For instance, the Martinez family wears different colored T-shirts. Uncle Joe and Aunt Maria's clan—adults, children, grandchildren—all wear red T-shirts while Uncle Frank and Aunt Delores' family wear blue T-shirts. A poster displayed in a prominent place shows a family tree indicating the different branches drawn in colors corresponding to the family T-shirt colors. Once the color system is memorized, you know at a glance whose grandchildren are playing on the swings. Family physical characteristics become easier to spot when you can mentally put all the family members together. This adds interest to your reunion and helps people get to know more about each other.

You can design your own special reunion shirts using plain colored T-shirts and permanent magic markers, or using the many decorating materials available in fabric or craft stores. Decorating T-shirts during the reunion could be an enjoyable activity for both kids and adults.

Aside from T-shirts, families might opt for wearing matching baseball caps, jackets, etc. You can be as elaborate or as simple in your identification process as you choose.

Name Tags. The most often used form of identification is the name tag. The name-of-the-game with name tags is not just identification, but *easy* identification. Make the letters large and clear enough to be read 6 feet away without squinting. Buy large felt-tip pens for this purpose and find someone who can print well, or have them printed on a computer printer. Letters $\frac{1}{4}$" high should be the minimum size, $\frac{3}{8}$" is better.

✓ Make name tags in advance for everyone who is registered.

✓ Have all necessary items for making name tags at the reunion. Assign someone to make them on the spot for last minute drop-ins or re-make any that have errors.

✓ The stick-on type of name tag won't last more than one day. Use the pin-on or clip-on type for multi-day events.

✓ "Button" name tags look nice, make nice souvenirs, and can have a family crest on them. But the standard size (2 $\frac{1}{4}$") is too small to be read easily. A more readable size is 2 $\frac{3}{4}$" which can be rather expensive.

Alternatives to Name Tags. As a unique alternative to the commonplace "peel-and-wear" tag, Virginia Graboyes of Vallejo, CA, painted a family tree on a big banner (Figure 10). The family has six branches, one for each of Mr. Graboyes' brothers, sisters, and their offspring. Each person was listed on the tree with his or her name on a leaf. Each family branch had leaves of a distinctive color. The beauty of this family tree is that the leaves were detachable name tags. For instance, if your grandfather was Stephen, your leaf was red. If your grandfather was Forrest, your leaf was orange, etc. When you removed your leaf to wear your name tag, a permanent leaf below the removeable name tag also showed your name. After everyone had arrived and was sporting name tags, a complete family tree on a banner was revealed for all to see—and everyone was identified by his or her name tag. The name tags were covered with clear contact paper so they would hold up through the several-day reunion.

FIGURE 10. Combination family tree and name tag dispenser.

The organizer of another reunion also created a unique name tag; one that ended up as a souvenir. She cut dry cedar branches into one-fourth inch slices, creating circles three inches in diameter. In the top of each circle of wood, she drilled two small holes and inserted yarn long enough to hang the circle around one's neck. The yarn was color coded for different families.

At the reunion, she set up a table with sandpaper, colored pens, and a clear lacquer spray. After families arrived and were settled for the three-day event, people visited the craft table and made their own name tags. On the tag, people wrote their names, hometowns, and year of the reunion. Everyone participated—from the youngest to the oldest—sanding, applying names, and adding other features to individualize their art. As families arrived, children who already had made their name tags took the new families to the craft table and instructed the newcomers on how to make theirs. They loved this duty, feeling an important part of the family and the reunion. Many saved their name tags as a memento of the special time spent together.

Obviously, like T-shirts, creating name tags can be a rewarding do-it-yourself project. If your reunion is several days long, this is a good first day "get acquainted" activity.

Decorations (or Don't Get Carried Away)

Decorations are always nice, but aren't absolutely necessary at reunions. You can go without, or you can keep them simple, tasteful, relatively inexpensive, and still maintain the spirit of the reunion. Most commonly used decorations are flower arrangements, flags, banners, balloons, and family crests incorporated into place settings and tablecloths. Floral arrangements make nice table centerpieces; however, they are a bit more expensive than balloons. Bud vases with a few bright flowers are attractive and sometimes cheaper.

If you are thinking about fancy do-it-yourself decorations, consider whether your group has someone with talent, interest, energy, and the ability to recruit and motivate helpers. Next, consider the cost and budget. Decorations are no longer a nickel-and-dime expense. If the interest and expertise is available in your group, then be sure to draw up a carefully itemized list of materials needed. At a large reunion, an "all-out" decoration job with flowers on each table, banners, crepe paper streamers, imprinted balloons and napkins, etc., can easily run $300–400. If this is the "look" you want, then it may be well worth the time and money spent.

Before launching a full-scale production, find out the facility's rules about decorating. Some indoor places don't allow thumb tacks or tape; others will allow masking tape, but no thumb tacks. Such rules may limit you to table center-pieces and banners. If a banquet facility allows you to decorate, the room may be available only an hour or two beforehand. This may severely limit your decorating plans or require a team effort. Consider how much help you will need. No matter how talented, one or two people may only be able to do a limited job in two hours. Also consider who is going to take them down and find out how soon after the event they must be removed.

If available in your area, you can have helium balloon bouquets delivered or you can rent helium tanks and inflate them yourself. Count the number of tables and figure four-to-seven latex balloons with one mylar (foil) balloon in the middle for a nice looking centerpiece. You can write or draw on the foil balloon (easiest when not inflated) in colored ink using marking pens. The super-large markers work best for this. You can use colored gift wrapping ribbon for "string" or the flashy metallic mylar ribbon available in party supply stores. The balloons should be tied to a decorative weighted object that is placed in the center of the table. Make this weighted object (the part that rests on the table) small enough so that during the meal you have room for food and utensils. Some balloon companies use large jingle bells for this purpose. The helium balloons themselves will rise up out of the way and present no problem.

Dessert cakes, just large enough to feed the people at each table, make nice centerpieces. Appropriate words and crests can be used to decorate the cakes. Numbers and letters made of sugar can be purchased at dime stores, drug stores, or supermarkets.

Pennants and banners can be made from butcher paper and poster paint. You can embellish them with crepe paper and glue-on stars or glitter which come in many colors. If you are having a group photo taken, a banner can also serve for identification purposes in the picture.

Imprinted Tableware. Napkins and coasters imprinted with the family name and/or crest can add a classy touch. You can see samples and order these from most stores that sell wedding, graduation, or prom items and supplies. Also try greeting card stores. If you can't find a store near you, call Carlson

FIGURE 11. Learn the rules before purchasing decorating material.

Craft (507/625-5011) and ask for their customer service department. Carlson is a wholesaler that supplies many small stores around the country, but they don't sell directly to the consumer. Ask for their representative nearest you who has a Graduation Album or an All Occasion Album. These albums have the styles and colors that you are looking for. Some stores have only the Wedding Album which isn't as useful for your purposes.

A visit to a party supply store will give you more ideas. In the Yellow Pages see "Balloons, Novelty and Toy, Retail," "Party Equipment, Renting," and "Party Supplies."

Using Music Effectively

Background music does not normally play an important role in family reunions. However, it can be used effectively. For example, something light, friendly, and "welcoming" during arrival time can set a "fun" mood. It could simply be recorded music, or perhaps a pianist, or a strolling guitarist. Other possibilities: a string quartet; ethnic music such as Irish, reggae, salsa, klezmer, Cajun, mariachi; country or bluegrass.

The menu of musical options is wide since it covers everything from recorded music to a full orchestra, as well as hundreds of types of music. Of course, a lot will be determined by your budget. Can you afford a large band or will you have to settle for a small band, a single musician, a disk jockey, recorded music, or musicians from within your own group?

Before deciding, investigate all options and costs. A reputable talent or music agency can tell you of the local talent available, and can be a lifesaver in case of problems.

Here are some ideas that have worked at family reunions:

✓ An ethnic band during arrival time.
✓ Special music pertaining to a chosen theme or era.
✓ Strolling strings.
✓ A rock band for a teen dance.
✓ A DJ and appropriate music for an adult's dance.
✓ An a capella singing group.
✓ A barbershop quartet.
✓ A rented jukebox with appropriate music.
✓ Accordion music during registration.
✓ A song leader inspiring people to sing well-known favorites.
✓ A family musical group.

FIGURE 12. Vasquez Family mariachi band, Williams, AZ.

If you hire professionals, have a back-up plan in case of bad weather, power failures, no-shows, etc. Identify all technical requirements, such as staging, chairs, sound systems, storage and security of instruments, unloading area, changing room, and refreshments in the changing room.

Choosing a Band. If it's a band you want, then there are two key considerations: The kind of music and the amount you want to pay. Most bands require a deposit and a contract. Be sure to reconfirm the engagement a week or two before the reunion. Rates vary widely from $200–300 for an inexperienced three-person group to $1500 or more for a large, established group. The average price is around $300–500 (1992).

Check the Yellow Pages under "Entertainers," "Musicians," or "Orchestras and Bands"; in the white pages look up "Musicians' Union." The people who manage bands and DJ's are called booking agents, and can be found under "Entertainment Bureaus" or "Professional Talent Management."

FIGURE 13. This group performed during their family reunion and included a special song written for the occasion.

Disk Jockeys (DJ's) are usually used at dances, though they can also provide background or theme music. A good DJ has a tape collection of thousands of songs, amazingly sophisticated equipment, and is able to play music from almost any era, as well as take requests. Most of them have lists of the top ten songs for any month and year, and a reference system that allows them to find, cue up, and play any request in a matter of seconds. Remember, it's a lot easier to tell a DJ to keep the volume down than a band. The best thing about having a DJ is that you get to hear the exact rendition of the song you remember, rather than a band's interpretation. For nostalgic purposes, this can be an important consideration.

There are people in almost every community who work as disk jockeys for events such as reunions, dances, and parties. Their rates vary between $300 and $500 per event (1992). Rates below $200 should be viewed with some skepticism; check on what you are actually getting. We strongly urge you to talk to groups that have hired the prospective DJ in the past. Speak with the person who was directly in charge of music for the group. For disk jockeys, look in the Yellow Pages under "Entertainers."

FIGURE 14. Disk Jockeys are popular at special dances during family reunions. They can play the exact rendition of the song you have in mind and they can control the volume, making it easier to converse.

Taped Music. In between events and while people are socializing, taped music provides a nice background. It could be music that holds special significance for the family, such as ethnic songs, or songs that were popular when many of the adults were young. Very few commercial records or tapes can give you the variety you will want, so try to tape individual selections from private collections. Since many people have kept their old records over the years, mention this need in your mailers. Audiotapes are convenient to play, but records are best because they make it easier to find requests—tapes being more difficult to cue up. If you decide to provide your own music in this way, have one person in charge of music, and acting as DJ.

Cassette tapes. Played on a home stereo or boom box, audio-tapes will provide good music in most situations. However, for a dance in a large room, such a system may not have enough wattage (power). The only way to test this is to try it in the room beforehand, but even this is tricky because in a real situation you have "crowd noise" to contend with and bodies absorbing the sound. "Auditorium sized" amplifiers and speakers can be rented, and some DJ's offer a "sound system only" for considerably less cost than their usual package.

Reunion Activities

To really enjoy a reunion, people need the opportunity to spend time with as many different family members as possible. Those who know each other well, and don't get to visit often, will usually get right down to the old fashioned gab fest. Those who do not know each other well, and those who see each other less frequently, often find structured activities helpful.

To facilitate contact and sharing, plan some organized activities that draw people together, yet not so many that the activities themselves become the main focus. There needs to be a balance between organized and free time. There should be activities, for example, that are available with no obligation to take part. Obviously, multi-day reunions need more planned activities than one-day reunions.

Young people have a more enjoyable time if things are planned for them. In fact, this is so important that Chapter 9 is devoted exclusively to children's activities. The following section covers primarily adult activities.

We would like to recommend an excellent book which lists hundreds of reunion activities for all ages: *Fun & Games for Family Gatherings* by Adrienne Anderson of Alberta, Canada, is a *must* for any serious family reunion planner. See p. 214 for more information.

Activity Check List. The following is a check list of possible activities for a family reunion. Don't assume you must accomplish all of these. Some are necessary for any reunion; others can be saved for future reunions if you don't presently have the resources or experience; others are only for very large reunions. We leave the choices to your discretion. For more children's activities, see Chapter 9.

✓ welcoming reception
✓ hospitality time to help first-timers get acquainted
✓ tours
✓ games, hikes
✓ campfire, songs
✓ continental breakfast
✓ group photos
✓ memorial service, wreath laying
✓ after dinner dance
✓ teen dance with disk jockey
✓ viewing old family movies, videos, and slides
✓ collecting information for genealogies or family histories
✓ collecting family health history
✓ raffles/auctions
✓ sale of merchandise
✓ awards, honors
✓ talent show
✓ professional entertainment
✓ program
✓ farewell brunch or breakfast

Activity Centers

A visiting area. Reunion activities help those attending achieve their basic goals: catching up with the events in other's lives, doing something enjoyable together, and learning more about the family. A quiet place where people can visit and get to know those long-lost cousins is a must. Place this area near a display of family memorabilia, complete with old photos, albums, diaries, a map showing attendees' hometowns, family tree, war medals, genealogies in progress and already published, and old letters. Family members can browse through this area at their leisure. You can have a slide projector and screen to show slides, or a VCR and monitor to show family videos. Make sure family possessions donated for this center are carefully labeled and one person is responsible for receiving, displaying, and returning the items. If you are concerned about documents or old photos being taken, place heavy clear plastic over everything on a table and tape the edges to the underside of the table.

FIGURE 15. Family memorabilia adds interest to the reunion.

A message center. At a large reunion, it's important to have a bulletin board (plus paper, pencils, and thumb tacks) for the exchange of personal messages. Messages from the reunion committee are posted on a separate, nearby bulletin board.

Refreshments. Many people in social situations need something to do with their hands and their mouths (other than talk) in order to feel at ease. Unfortunately, alcohol consumption often fills this role, especially if liquor is the only thing available. Also serve chips and dip, nuts, sodas, fruit juice and coffee, and other "finger food."

Special presentations. Families interested in learning how to record their history could have a speaker from a local genealogy society or a certified genealogist discuss how to collect and write their genealogy and family history. Those already knowledgeable in genealogical research might engage a speaker who has more sophisticated information about an area where early relatives settled or the "old country" from which the kin immigrated. Attendance at this type of program should, of course, not be mandatory. See the Appendix for ways to contact local genealogists.

Slides/movies/old photos. People enjoy looking at their past. You can set aside in a corner a slide projector, a screen, and a table or bulletin board with old photos. In your mailers ask people to bring old photos and movies to the reunion and assign a volunteer to show slides or movies three or four times during the reunion (once is never enough). A projector that automatically cycles slides can be set up for a continuous showing. Don't forget an extra projection bulb and an extension cord. For safety purposes, tape all cords to the floor or carpet with duct tape.

You should also consider keeping a scrapbook of each reunion. These will become more and more interesting over the years. For a source of unique, high quality scrapbooks and photo albums, see the Appendix.

Have people put their names on the items they bring (provide materials for this) and remind them to pick up their things before they leave.

Residence map. A map like the one in Figure 16 gives a good overview of the group's geographical mix, and besides it's fun to see where everybody lives. To create the map, you will need a map of the United States and Canada (be sure it includes Hawaii and Alaska, if necessary), stick-pins (use different colors for different families), and a board you can stick pins into. Tape the map to the board (cork or cardboard). For large groups, have people insert a stick pin where they live. With small groups, write or type the family's name on labels, attach each label to a pin, and stick the pin in the appropriate place. Be sure to have a large table to use for this display or it could be hung on a wall.

Create a family store. See Chapter 3 for a full explanation of the family store and other fund-raising activities.

Make a quilt together. Families that like to quilt can have a quilt frame set up at the reunion so that anyone who wants to participate can add their stitches. Each year a different family brings their quilt top for the project. Or some families ask for

FIGURE 16. Residence maps are always interesting.

quilt blocks to either produce a group quilt to be auctioned or to trade blocks with others.

In the Kenny clan, each family designed a quilt block depicting something about themselves. They made as many copies of their block as there were families in the clan. At the reunion, they traded blocks. Each family then had enough blocks for their own copy of the family quilt. Subsequent reunions were spent putting the quilts together for each family. Men, women, and children all participated and the gab fests around the quilt frame drew the family closer together. Even the letters sent back and forth during the planning stages created new family closeness. See directions for children creating a paper quilt in Chapter 9.

Gathering for a Program

Be sure to have at least a short program where all the clan can get together and share. It's a great way to introduce everyone. It can take place in a formal setting with chairs or informally around a campfire. At large reunions, it can follow the main meal. Often the oldest family member in each branch will introduce his or her family and announce births, engagements, marriages, deaths, special awards, graduations, appointments, etc. All these milestones create a sense of history as well as pride in the accomplishments of the kin. *Everyone is included; everyone is important.*

Here are some possibilities for your program:

✓ **Acknowledgements.** You may want to thank the organizing committee, and perhaps single out one or two people who worked especially hard. A small gift may or may not be appropriate; use your discretion.

A more formal acknowledgement could be made by presenting an engraved plaque, trophy, or a quality gift. Possible candidates for such an award are the reunion founder, a family elder, someone who has never missed a reunion, your "historian" who finally finished the family history, or anyone who has distinguished himself or herself in some way.

✓ **Awards.** Here are some possibilities for awards: Who traveled the farthest? Who has the most children? Who is the youngest grandparent? Who has the most great-grandchildren? Who has the most descendants present? Who has attended the most reunions? Who arrived first or last? The youngest/oldest present.

FIGURE 17. *At the Daniel Family reunion, a painted saw blade and a framed quilt square were awarded as prizes. The gifts were hand-made by family members.*

Prizes awarded for such achievements can be a family memento. Some families have special T-shirts, buttons, or caps. Food items and/or recipes are often given as prizes, such as a ham or watermelon, or Aunt Mindy's prize winning jam. You may have a craftsman in your family who would make a treasured award, as in Figure 17.

Clever or humorous awards are a tradition for many families. Remember, your goal is not to embarrass anyone, but for the whole group to have a good laugh at itself. One family gave the parents of the most children a shoe with many tiny dolls tied all over it. See the Appendix for a source of joke awards.

If you ask the right questions, much of the information needed to pick the recipients for your awards can come from the surveys sent out in the mailers. However, be prepared to make some last-minute changes based on surveys filled out at the reunion itself. Also, you will discover that some categories will require direct observation ("last to arrive") and perhaps a few discreet questions asked during the reunion. Someone must be assigned to this task. "The Survey" in Chapter 5 will give you more information.

✓ **Prizes.** Door prizes and other special gifts are always fun, but the process of choosing a winner should be quick and easy. The most common way to choose a winner is to place a special sticker on the bottom of a saucer (which is easy to look under, unlike a plate or cup which may contain food or beverage). (Placing it under a chair can cause a tremendous disruption as people get up to turn their chairs over.) For multiple prizes, have multiple stickers with different numbers or colors.

✓ **Toasts.** A toast is never necessary at a reunion, but if done right, can be quite moving and meaningful. The length of a good toast varies anywhere from a few words to a few minutes, though the shorter ones tend to be better. The person giving the toast should be nothing less than "completely willing" to do the job. An appropriate time for a toast would be right after the meal or at the end of the program just before everyone gets up. Of course, everyone should have a glass with a bit of "spirits" in it—either wine or an after-dinner liqueur. Grape juice, non-alcoholic wine, or sparkling cider would also be appropriate for nondrinkers and for the children. Most facilities will allow you

to bring your own wine for "toasting purposes." This will save you money, but check first; and don't forget the corkscrew.

✓ **Speeches.** The rule of thumb is to keep them short or not have them at all. People bore easily, especially the children. An interesting exception is noted in the adjacent photo. This is John L. Lillibridge III posing as his immigrant ancestor, Thomas Lillibridge (1660–1724) at the family reunion in 1991. John's special presentation was not previously announced. He was dressed in the costume of the day and his 10 minute speech was set in the language of the early 1700's. He talked about his family and his life in America. Many of his descendants wanted their picture taken with him.

✓ **Announcements.** While you have a captive audience, use your time well. Remind people to buy raffle tickets, visit the family store, donate for the upcoming family history book, participate in planned activities, etc. Let people know who is in charge of the mailing list and remind them to send change-of-addresses to that person.

In Memoriam

A *memorial service* can be held in remembrance of the lineage of our families, and perhaps as special farewell to those who have passed away since the last reunion. At a family reunion, there are several appropriate ways of honoring the deceased: a short prayer during the main program, a moment of silence before any event, a memorial breakfast or brunch during which there is a short service, a wreath-laying ceremony at a nearby chapel, memorial, gravesite, or family cemetery. A family or local minister, or a family elder could be asked to say a few words.

There are many ways to arrange an *altar or memorial display.* It's important to keep it tasteful and carefully prepared. When possible, have photographs of the deceased. Give each photo or each name its own "space." Flowers are always appropriate. Votive candle(s) are a nice touch if the local fire codes allow it. If indoors, there could be a soft spotlight setting off the whole display. The important thing is that it should be by itself with no other display or distraction nearby.

Planning for Emergencies

It's important to consider possible on-site emergencies, especially for older people. An illness can be brought on or complicated by change in diet, drinking, time-zone changes, fatigue, excitement, weather, and altitude. Be sure to have a plan to cover emergencies, especially for longer reunions.

Become familiar with local medical support systems. For instance, does the city have a 911 number to call? Get the number for the police and nearest hospital. How about a dentist who can be contacted on the weekends or on short notice? Who in your group is CPR trained? Is there a first aid kit handy? Where is it? Where can you rent a wheelchair? Is there a 24-hour drugstore nearby? How does the hotel initiate emergency service? Know what the system is and how it works. It is always better to err on the side of caution than to risk inadequate care and treatment. In order for everyone to have access to key emergency numbers, consider publishing them in the program or separate flyer.

Tipping

Tipping can be an important part of a reunion; professional meeting planners know this, but, unfortunately, many reunion organizers do not. For this reason the quality of service at some reunions can be lacking. If your reunion site is a hotel or resort, these tips on tipping are especially appropriate:

✓ Assume you will tip and budget for it.

✓ Alert your reunion staff to look for and remember people who provide exceptional service, then tip accordingly.

✓ Good rule: Expect good service, tip exceptional service. Do

not tip in advance. Possible exception: bellmen, front desk
personnel.

✓ Tips do not all have to be in cash. A small gift or letter of
commendation are both acceptable.

✓ If "automatic gratuities" are written into your contract,
know exactly what they are for and who gets them so that
you do not double tip.

✓ Certain positions should not be tipped: general manager,
directors of departments, anyone in sales or management.

✓ If, after you get home, you realize you forgot someone, send
a tip with a note. It's never too late to recognize good service.

CHAPTER 8

Feeding the Family

The Big Question – Letting Someone Else Cook – Buffets and Sit Down Meals – Bringing Your Own Food – Stretch Your Food Dollars – Serving and Clean Up – Keep a History – A Banquet Checklist.

The Big Question

Feeding a large reunion group with a minimum of fuss requires careful planning. But first, ask yourself one question: *Are you going to provide your own food or hire someone else to do the cooking?* Your decision may well be tied to finances, since a caterer or restaurant usually costs much more than preparing your own reunion meal(s). If the gathering will take place over several days, you may want to have different options for different meals. For example, you could let people find their own breakfasts, get together for a large noon meal, and later split into smaller groups that provide their own dinners.

Letting Someone Else Cook

If you decide to hire someone to do the cooking, survey different caterers and restaurants in the area to get an idea of what they charge. Some church groups, hotels, granges, or similar organizations also do catering. The local Chamber of Commerce may know of civic groups that will provide meals and facilities.

Create a list of all the information you need to provide a caterer when asking for an estimate. This list should include the date and time of the event (caterers may be completely booked a year ahead at certain times of year, *e.g.*, for June weddings or Christmas parties), approximately how many adults and children you're expecting, and the type of meal and beverages you would prefer.

When getting estimates or meal prices, be sure to give each caterer or restaurant the *same* information, reading from your list. This way you're sure to "compare apples with apples." Take extensive notes when talking to different caterers so you don't have to rely on memory when deciding which to hire.

Use a separate page in your notebook for each restaurant or caterer, heading it with the appropriate name, address, and phone number. Follow with the date you phoned and the name and title of the person you spoke to. (Make sure that you speak to the person in charge of group reservations.)

Here are a few important issues to cover with restaurants and caterers:

✓ Ask about their policy on deposits and cancellations.

✓ Request the names of two references you can call to make sure everything promised on other occasions was successfully delivered.

✓ If you are planning to serve alcoholic beverages before or with the meal, be sure you know the facility's policy. Some places forbid alcohol, while others allow you to bring your own—at considerable savings.

✓ Is the restaurant easy to find? This is especially important if you have lots of out-of-towners attempting to locate it, especially if your reunion meal is at night. It may be wise to select a place near your lodging.

✓ Does the restaurant have adequate parking?

✓ Is the restaurant or hall located in a safe neighborhood?

✓ Does the restaurant have easy access and restrooms for persons in wheelchairs?

✓ How many highchairs or booster seats do they have?

✓ Do they provide flowers or other decorations? (See the section on decorating, p. 79.)

When you've collected enough information to make a reasonable choice, it's a good idea to visit the restaurant or banquet hall and look at the actual room *before* making the deposit. If the event is to be in the evening, visit in the evening. Observe the interior and exterior lighting, the distance from the parking lot to the front door, and so on. To check out the ambiance and the friendliness of the personnel, it's best to eat a meal during your visit (without mentioning that you're "scouting").

When you do make a reservation, request a written confirmation letter including all the details you've agreed upon, such as the date and time, menu, number of persons expected, and price per person. Review this letter very carefully and phone your contact person immediately if you find any discrepancies.

Assuming that you're making reservations six months to a year in advance, you should phone the contact person two months before the event, and again one week before, to make sure everything is proceeding smoothly. Make sure you know exactly what is expected of you—if anything—prior to the actual meal.

Buffets and Sit Down Meals

Generally, a buffet-style meal with several kinds of dishes can offer appetizing choices for everyone, even the vegetarians and dieters. Include salads, hot entrees such as lasagna (some of them meatless), meats, rolls, fresh fruit, and desserts. Buffets also reduce the need for servers; however, you may want some servers replenishing the serving dishes, removing empty dishes, circulating among tables, providing and replenishing beverages, and generally tidying up.

When it comes to organizing, a "sit-down" meal involves more work than a buffet. If you opt for a "sit-down" meal, offer several choices (*e.g.*, entrees featuring meat, chicken, fish, or vegetarian), and you must tell the restaurant how many diners have chosen each entree. Guests select their entrees when they make reservations for the reunion, marking choices on a card they return with their checks. This way, the restaurant is given an exact meal count well before the event. Keep duplicate records—and bring them to the reunion—in case people forget what they ordered.

Or you can offer only one menu for the sit-down meal. This is easier on the organizers although less accommodating to guests. The restaurant you choose may have a particular specialty (such as prime rib) which becomes the reunion dinner entree. This option can work well if the restaurant has a substantial salad bar, so that vegetarians, small children, and dieters can find plenty to eat while skipping the entree. If such selective dining is acceptable to the restaurant, ask if they offer a two-tiered pricing system, dividing those who choose the entree from those who eat only the salad, bread, and dessert.

When talking to caterers and restaurant staff, be sure to tell them about any special dietary and/or religious restrictions which could present problems. For example, if many reunion members are elderly, you can anticipate that they'd prefer a low-salt, low-fat, low-sugar meal. If you expect a lot of young children, you need to consider their tastes. (Along that line, providing a loaf of sliced bread and the ubiquitous peanut butter and jelly may head off a tantrum or two.)

Bringing Your Own Food

Cooking your own reunion feast is certainly more work, but home cooking provides a personal touch that few restaurants can match. The key here—to avoid complaints like "I did all the work..."—is to make sure the jobs and expenses are equitably distributed.

The easiest—and, therefore, the most popular—approach is to have a *potluck*, where everyone contributes food to share. You could encourage people to bring special family dishes— such as Uncle Harry's barbequed ribs or Grandma Parker's strawberry/rhubarb pie—along with written recipes for each dish. These recipes can be incorporated into a special keepsake cookbook (see p. 34). To add interest, label each dish at the potluck ("Aunt Liza's Pickled Beets").

However, to make sure a potluck doesn't end up consisting of 26 salads, you need to organize who brings which items. The best way to cover all the bases is to make a master list of everything essential to the meal. To avoid forgetting something major, it helps to run this list by at least three friends—or get them to help you prepare it in the first place.

The system of using last names "beginning with A–F bring salads" won't work for a family reunion since many people will have the same last name. Using first names can also create confusion—whose first names do you use? Instead, *assign* salads, main dishes, desserts, beverages, breads, fruits, etc. Be sure to keep track of what everyone is bringing.

Remember, people traveling long distances will find it easier to bring something from a nearby supermarket instead of dragging a casserole across the country. These out-of-towners can be assigned items such as ice, paper plates, cups and napkins, plastic utensils, charcoal and lighter fluid if you're barbequing, beverages, fresh fruit, meats, hamburger and hotdog rolls, mustard, ketchup, and other condiments.

Some important items you may want to put on your potluck list include:

✓ **Decorations**—either for the serving tables or the tables where people are eating. Is someone in the family eager to show off his or her roses? Family gardeners near the reunion site may be a good source for flowers. How about something big and striking—like a flag representing the family's ethnic origin or a welcoming banner—hanging above your serving table? Children are a good resource for imaginative drawings—and may pass rainy afternoons for months before the reunion drawing pictures on paper tablecloths or creating suitable centerpieces. Also see the section on decorating, p. 79.

✓ **Condiments**—list all that are needed for the items you are serving, starting with the easily-forgotten salt and pepper.

✓ **Equipment for your cooking area**—if there is to be one—and for last-minute preparations. A couple of cutting boards and some sharp knives are essential. And how about barbeque gear such as tongs, potholders, and aprons? Don't forget the matches.

✓ **Extra seating**—it can be comfortable folding lawn chairs, rented chairs, or bales of hay. Don't forget highchairs or booster seats.

✓ **Miscellaneous equipment**—those items needed to keep food and drink cold or hot. You may need to rent or borrow a coffee urn or a big punch bowl. Ice-filled washbuckets and ice chests are useful to keep beverages cold and prevent perishables from spoiling.

✓ **Shelter**—if it's an outdoor event, will you need to rent some sort of tent or pavilion in case of rain or for shade?

✓ **Cleanup gear,** such as detergent, scouring pads, sponges, paper towels, dish drainers, and large washtubs may be needed. Don't forget brooms and dustpans.

There are several popular variations on the "potluck" approach. One is to have people bring their own meat to barbeque, while the salads, desserts, rolls, and other side dishes are assigned in potluck fashion, or are provided by the committee. Another approach is to have guests contribute money (the amount based on the number of adults and children attending) to a general fund, from which the Reunion Committee buys meat to barbeque, charcoal, ice, beverages, utensils and paper plates, etc., The salads and desserts are contributed via potluck. If you choose this option make sure to collect everyone's money *before* the reunion.

Even if most of the food is purchased by your committee, you can still ask guests to bring one special dish to be judged in a contest. It's fun to ask the family to vote for their favorite, awarding an appropriate gift (an apron, chef's hat, potholders, etc.) to the elected Champion Cook(s). Provide a ballot box, small paper ballots, and a couple of pencils tied to the box with strings. Ask people to vote after they've finished eating (including desserts) and appoint a committee of older children to run the election, tally the votes, and hand out the prize(s).

Other types of potlucks are limited only by your imagination and the location of the reunion. You can have a "chili cookoff," where many variations of that specialty simmer all day, with the committee providing cold drinks, corn bread, and ice cream or watermelon for dessert. Or tie your meal to an event such as a clam dig. The clams go into huge pots of chowder with different family members providing the remaining ingredients (bacon, onions, celery, milk, bottled clam juice, parsley, sherry, etc.). Don't forget the garlic bread, drinks and desserts.

Depending on where you hold your reunion, there may be other regional favorites that influence your menu. Let's say one family lives on a ranch and offers to roast a whole pig. This porker becomes the focal point for a theme meal—whether it's an Hawaiian Luau or a Cowboy Cookout.

Don't overlook the particular cooking talents and/or generosity of someone in your group when planning the meal. The makings for a great reunion meal and setting may be right under your nose.

Little details can also shape your meal into something more fun and more memorable than the usual potluck. For example, a Luau theme will be a lot more convincing if you hire a ukelele player (or obtain taped Polynesian music), ask people to wear Hawaiian-style flowered shirts, buy paper leis and have them handed out by a child dressed in a grass skirt, serve drinks with little paper parasols in them, make some fake palm trees from painted cardboard or plywood, and haul in some sand for a photo backdrop.

Stretch Your Food Dollars

✓ If you are having your reunion at a hotel, don't ask what they charge for the meal. *Tell* them how much you wish to spend per meal and have them prepare a meal accordingly. If necessary, eliminate desserts and extra vegetables. Ask the chef about special food buys, food on hand, and concurrent meals with other groups.

✓ If unsure of attendance, select "stretchables" such as pastas and stews.

✓ Avoid delicacies such as shrimp, lobster, crab, and caviar unless you are in an area where the prices are reasonable.

FIGURE 18. Same reunion, different meals.

Serving and Clean Up

Whatever kind of meal you're creating, don't forget to give some thought to serving and cleaning up. Buffet style is certainly the easiest way to serve a crowd. Set up your buffet tables so that people can access the food from both sides at once, serving themselves faster. Some older children really enjoy helping and can be mobilized for serving beverages or desserts.

When laying out your serving area, be sure to include several beverage stations for easy access. Cold sodas, mineral waters, juices, and nonalcoholic drinks should be separated from the beer and alcoholic drinks. Provide recycling boxes for aluminum and glass containers.

It's easier to serve and clean up a buffet if it's in a slightly different location than the pre-meal snacks and the desserts. Separate them so they don't create traffic jams if groups are serving themselves from different tables at the same time.

Be sure to appoint a cleanup committee which oversees the details of trash pick up and disposal, making sure all fires are out, utensils washed, and so on. If you're using a rented facility, such as a campground or hall for your meal, the return of the security deposit is often dependent upon a good cleanup job. One person (Chairman of Cleanup) should be assigned to do a final site inspection and collect the deposit, turning it over to the Reunion Committee's Treasurer.

Keep a History

Soon after the reunion is over, whether you used a caterer, restaurant, or the wits and generosity of your own family for the group meal(s), it's a good idea to haul out that dog-eared notebook again and write down what worked and what didn't. This is the best time to record your thoughts about how you would do it differently next time. You may want to solicit opinions of several others for this analysis. Your notes, however brief, will be of tremendous help to the next person (even if it's you) who feeds the group.

A Banquet Checklist

Here is a check list for a large banquet:

✓ When, during the reunion, will the banquet be held?

✓ Size of the room: seating capacity, dance floor space, etc.

✓ How will you be charged by the facility: signed guarantee, collected tickets, or by quantities? Remember, it's your job to know the number of people that will attend, and you should assume the burden of incorrect projections.

✓ Taxes and gratuities.

✓ Decorations. Ask if the site has table decorations in stock.

✓ Flowers: what type, size and how many?

✓ Entertainment: band, DJ, taped music, space to perform, staging.

✓ Rental equipment, costs.

✓ Check on local liquor laws. Some regulations may affect you. Some counties are dry, or are dry on certain days.

✓ Alcohol controls. Types of bars: host, cash, your own. Will you sell tickets? Bartender to guest ratio: 1 to 75 is average.

✓ Time span of the event. When is dinner to be served? When will the meal end?

✓ Will there be a reception? Will you need a separate room?

✓ Give the facility manager a diagram of what the room should look like set up.

✓ Type and color of linen you will use.

✓ Audio-visual equipment.

✓ Will there be a head table? Who will sit there?

✓ Type of dress.

✓ Smoking, no smoking?

✓ Who will collect tickets?

✓ Signs for event.

✓ Dressing room for musicians.

✓ Type of service: buffet, individual plates.

✓ Menu: variety, creativity, cost?

✓ Are vegetables canned, frozen, or fresh? Accept only fresh, maybe frozen.

✓ Special dietary requirements? Vegetarian, low sodium, low fat, no sugar, no wheat, religious.

✓ Waiter-to-guest ratio? This can mean fast or slow service. (No greater than 1 to 20 for plated meals.)

✓ Distribution of materials: menu cards, programs, favors.

✓ How will guests be admitted to the room?

✓ Will you need security?

✓ Room lighting, electricity, spotlights, public address system?

✓ Parking.

✓ Checkroom for coats?

✓ Location of rest rooms.

✓ Photography/video coverage. Costs? Instructions for how to obtain photos or tapes.

✓ What other events will be going on at the facility simultaneous to your event?

CHAPTER 9

Showing the Kids a Good Time

*Continuing the Tradition – Means of Mixing – Site Selection –
Involving Kids in Family History – Indoor Activities – Getting
Serious About Games – Special Reunion Games – Some Family
Favorites – Adapting Popular Games – Create Your Own Games.*

Continuing the Tradition

The greatest joy of a family reunion is also its greatest
challenge: bringing the generations together in such a way that
the youngsters are entertained and engaged, and thus will
want to continue the tradition as they mature. A family
reunion should be so enjoyable that the kids look forward to
each gathering as much as the adults, if not more so. For that
to happen, it's essential that they be enthusiastically included
and involved as much as possible, and not merely babysat or
herded off to where they won't bother the grown-ups.

Means of Mixing

Adult family members bring bountiful memories to share at a reunion. Young family members, often from distant corners of the country, need to find their *own* common ground in order for friendships to blossom. Nearly any topic will work as an ice-breaker when you're introducing youngsters to each other: a common interest in video games, in owning pets, in skateboarding, in collecting baseball cards, in popular music and television shows—anything they can talk about comfortably as they get to know each other.

The same is true in getting younger and older family members to know each other. A love of music, sports, nature, or other areas can be used to break the ice between relatives of disparate ages, and may eventually result in multi-generational musical jam sessions, nature hikes, and other spontaneous outgrowths of common interests. Croquet, by the way, is a great game for "mixing the ages."

One of the best and most important parts of a reunion for youngsters (and adults) is the building of common memories. This can be done both through organized group activities (hayrides, softball and volleyball games, relay races, family story-telling, a hiking or bicycling trip, a kids-only party with pizza and dancing, a skating party, card games, board games, drawing contests, etc.) and through casual encounters with each other. Ideally, the reunion experience should provide the kids with plenty of stories to tell their friends back home about all the neat things they did and the nifty cousins, aunts, and uncles they met at the reunion.

Adults love to kiss and pinch children's cheeks, and haggle over who the members of the newest generation most resemble in the family. However, such attention can be overwhelming for youngsters, particularly those who have never been to a reunion. Give kids plenty of space and time to get used to the crowd on their own terms. Don't assume that everyone's going to get along with everyone else at first sight just because they're related. It may take awhile for the kids to warm up to each other, as well as to adult relatives they've never met.

The different needs and interests of different age groups must be taken into consideration in planning a successful family reunion. Activities that delight preschoolers and kinder-garteners may bore or embarrass teenagers. Your best bet is to consult the experts—the kids themselves. Well ahead of time, send out a questionnaire to children of various age brackets, asking them to rate a list of activities they would find most in-teresting. Or solicit the advice of a few imaginative youngsters (one for each age bracket) about what they think they and their peers would most enjoy doing during the reunion.

Don't overstructure reunion activities, though. Everyone young and old should feel welcome, but not obliged to par-ticipate in any of a variety of outings and activities. For some youngsters, unstructured time spent with each other and some favorite elders may yield the best memories.

Babysitting. *Since many families make a reunion their family vacation for the year, it's important that it be a true vacation for every member of the family.* Don't expect teenagers to babysit the younger crowd, except for short stretches of time, and only if they really want to do it (for some teenage girls, this might be their favorite activity). Adolescent resentments can be kept to a minimum by hiring nonfamily babysitters to care for the wee ones who need close supervision, leaving the older kids free to come and go.

Site Selection (also see Chapter 1)

For family reunions lasting several days, it's a good idea to choose a location with a lot of recreational options, both at the reunion site and in the general vicinity. When you evaluate possible sites, keep in mind diversions that would have special appeal for young family members, as well as for chaperoning adults. The following list focuses on some considerations:

✓ Is there a theme park nearby? an amusement park? a zoo? a museum? a playground? a miniature golf course?

✓ A facility where bicycles, skates, canoes, rowboats, or other recreational equipment can be rented? a hiking trail?

✓ A public beach or pool with lifeguards? a lake suitable for fishing or waterskiing?

✓ A bowling alley for a rainy day?

✓ A shopping mall or interesting downtown area?

✓ A dairy farm or small factory (a place that makes its own chocolates, for instance) that would make a good field trip?

✓ *On the premises of your reunion site,* is there a swimming pool? a baseball diamond? a basketball hoop? a volleyball or badminton net, or at least a place to set one up?

✓ A piano? a stage (and maybe even a sound system) that can be used for a family talent show or family-history skit? a screen for showing family slides and home movies? a large-screen television for showing videos?

You don't need to have all of these options available, of course, but you *do* want to have enough diversions at hand, so you won't be confronted with that dreaded refrain of youth everywhere: "There's nothing to dooooo!!"

Involving Kids in Family History

Many children's activities can parallel the interests of the adults. If the family is genealogy oriented, the children can also have activities with this focus. To keep their interest, tracking down ancestors should be presented as a game or solving a mystery. Some families create their own versions of Trivial Pursuit or Jeopardy based on family history. Others make a treasure hunt list for the kids in which they have to collect pertinent information about relatives, living and dead.

Marielen and Anthony Christensen have written a book *Keeping Memories Alive,* which focuses on ways children can keep their own family and personal histories (see the Appendix for information on this book). Materials brought from home can be inserted into family scrap books, photographs traded, and stories written. Older children might like to make a video of the reunion. They can also interview older family members, recording the conversation on tape or in a handmade book.

Children of all ages can work together to make a family "quilt" by each decorating a paper square depicting a family memory. Finished squares are taped together or sewn with yarn into a big paper quilt to be displayed throughout the event and at future reunions. Learning to keep family history alive can be important in helping children understand and take pride in the accomplishments of the family.

Indoor Activities

If your reunion is held at the time of year when rain, snow, or cold may limit outdoor activity, children can spend time arranging special displays of their collections and crafts. Set up time can be part of their activity together. One of the mailers sent out prior to the reunion should request that children bring these materials.

Other indoor activities for children might include singing songs, playing instruments, planning skits or talent shows to be performed for the adults, playing cards, checkers, dominoes, board games, or Trivial Pursuit and Pictionary. Some adults may want to join in these activities, and should be encouraged to do so, as long as they don't dominate the games.

Another great way to entertain the youngsters indoors is with old home movies or slides taken when the adults were young. Adults can provide the narration or the children can take these movies and slides, put words to them, and put on a show. Children love to have an opportunity to tease adults and this provides them with the perfect vehicle while, at the same time, getting them interested in their common past.

Getting Serious About Games

Games seem to belong at family reunions like cotton candy at a county fair; they are great icebreakers and encourage people to join together. Just don't take them too seriously. The point is to have fun, rather than engage in cutthroat competition. Games and sports can be organized by age or skill level, or you can mix the age groups for a lesson in diversity and tolerance.

Some families organize traditional sports activities, such as softball, volleyball, golf, tennis, or soccer. Others hold team races or track meets. Grandparents and rural dwellers may remember such old-time games as sack races, three-legged races, wheelbarrow races, egg or water balloon toss, bobbing for apples, greased pole climbs, tug-of-war, and baby races. Most of these traditional American games are easy to learn and are very physical without being dangerous—a good way to wear out energetic kids!

The *sack race* is just like a regular foot race, but each contestant has to jump to the finish line in a gunnysack. For the *three-legged race*, put two roughly equal-size participants shoulder to shoulder, and tie their two inner ankles together with a piece of short, soft rope or a cloth belt. The contestants must run together to the finish line, which requires cooperation and coordination! In a *wheelbarrow race*, a large child or adult holds the ankles of a smaller person who "runs" forward on his or her hands.

For the *egg or balloon toss*, each person picks a partner. The partners line up facing each other. This creates two long parallel lines of participants who begin the toss while standing

a yard away from each other. Partners throw raw eggs or water balloons to each other with an underhand toss; everyone tosses at the same time. After each round of tossing, those partners whose egg or balloon survived take a step back and toss again. The others must drop out. The winners are the last two people to keep their egg or balloon from breaking.

All that's needed for a *greased pole climb* is a smooth vertical metal pole, a can of lard, and a piece of bright yarn to tie

around the pole. Grease the pole with the lard and tie the yarn high on the pole to provide a "goal" for climbers. (Another enticing goal is an envelope with money inside.) Kids take turns shinnying up the pole. There are all kinds of tricks to successful pole climbing. Experienced climbers use dirt, grass, bandannas, socks, and their own shirt sleeves to wipe the pole as they climb. Although the climb seems impossible at first, the smart athletes soon

FIG. 19. Greased pole climb.

FIGURE 20. Sack race (top) and wheelbarrow race.

refine their techniques and reach the goal. Obviously, this is not an activity for the faint-hearted or compulsively clean. Old clothes are a must for this game.

Tug-of-war can be played anywhere with a soft, strong rope. A good summertime variation is to play across a creek or through a stream of water from a hose. The losers get wet and everyone has a laugh. Don't use any type of rope that stretches a lot (like nylon). If such a rope breaks, it can snap like a large rubber band and hurt people.

Baby races are always fun. Put all family crawlers in a row with one parent. Put the other parent at the finish line and see which baby makes it first.

Some Special Reunion Games

Most of the families we surveyed wanted to include more games at their reunions. The only thing holding them back was a lack of good game ideas. Fortunately, there are some references available to help with game planning. The New Games Foundation (now defunct) created games focusing on participation, creativity, and community, and published two books, *The New Games Book,* and *More New Games* (out of print, try your library). Their games fit well with family reunions because their goal was to mingle, break the ice, get acquainted, and have fun. Some of their games require cooperation, while others are competitive. Some are for small groups, others for large. Their games are categorized as high, medium, or low activity. Most can be changed or adapted to your group's needs. Some require simple equipment such as frisbees or nerf balls. Many require none. No special field or gym is needed, and you don't have to worry about your physical condition or athletic ability. In other words, they are easy to play and can involve a wide range of ages and abilities.

Another great book is *Fun & Games for Family Gatherings,* which lists skits, stunts, mock fashion shows, words to songs, different types of races and hikes, projects, and much more. See the Appendix and p. 214 for more information.

Game 1: Family Treasure Hunt

To play "Family Treasure Hunt," prepare a list of requests or questions to answer. Distribute one copy to each player.

1. Find two people who traveled over 200 miles to the reunion: _____ and _____.

2. Find the mother with the most children: _____.

3. Find the oldest and youngest persons:_____ and _____.

4. How many children did Grandma Bertha have? _____.

5. Find three people who married into the family: _____, _____, and _____.

6. Find three children who presently are on a soccer or baseball team: _____, _____, and _____.

7. What country did great-grandfather Espinoza come from? _____.

8. Which relative used to work on a fishing boat? _____.

9. How long has the Nelson Farm been in the family? _____.

A list of 12 to 15 requests and/or questions is probably enough to keep everyone playing for 30 minutes. The players need a pencil or pen. Each player hunts for the person or persons who meet the requirements of the request or who can answer the question. The first person with all the blanks filled correctly wins. It's fun to read the answers to the whole group, identifying the persons listed by having them raise their hands. The whole group learns to identify each other in some special way.

One family that played this game gave the questions to the children while the adults were visiting. This kept the children busy seeking answers and the adults didn't mind an interuption from time to time by children searching for the person who could answer their questions.

Game 2: Who am I?

Create two teams of at least five players each. Players must be agile enough to run 20 feet. The age of the youngest participants depends on their ability to understand the game and join in.

One team is called the *Actors* and the other the *Guessers.* The *Actors* meet at a distance from the *Guessers* so their plans cannot be heard. One member of the *Actors* is chosen as the "subject" of the game. The team determines what they are going to act out in pantomime about the *Actor's* life that would identify him or her, such as an occupation or hobby.

When the *Actors* have planned their pantomime, the two teams line up behind opposing lines about 20 or more feet apart. The location of each starting line must be clearly defined. The *Actors* walk a few steps toward the *Guessers* yelling, "Here we come!" The *Guessers* also move forward asking, "Where from?" The *Actors* advance again shouting out the general geographical location of the subject's home. For example, if the *Actor* is from Los Angeles, the team might say "Southern California." If he or she is the only one on the team from Southern California, this clue would give the *Actor's* identify away immediately. Therefore, the *Actors* would name a larger geographical area, such as "California" or "west of the Rockies," to keep the *Guessers* guessing.

Then the *Guessers* advance to midway between the two starting lines and ask, "What is your trade?" The *Actors* come to the center line yelling, "We'll do a charade!" In pantomime, the *Actors* act out the hobby or occupation of the subject.

The *Guessers* must guess the occupation or hobby, and the *Actor* it belongs to. As soon as the *Guessers* have figured out both, they shout out their answer and chase the *Actors* back toward their line. Any *Actors* tagged before crossing their starting line must join the *Guessers* for the next round in which they become the *Actors*. The team with the largest number of members after a preset number of rounds wins. This game is good for "mixing" and learning about family members.

Game 3: Family Statistics

This game requires two teams of eight or more players. If all participants are agile, the age span can be 6 to 100. Someone in a wheelchair can participate if the game is played on a flat surface. You can play inside or outside, standing or seated (one chair required for each person). All you need is room for each team to line up.

The point of the game is to get your team lined up according to a single statistic or requirement, such as height, age, birthday order, astrological sign (from Aries to Pisces), distance traveled to the reunion, number of reunions attended, family birth order, alphabetical order by first or last names, city or state of origin, and so on. A leader who is not on either team selects the statistic. Statistics or requirements can be as complicated as the teams can comprehend.

The first team to get lined up according to the statistic or requirement yells out its order and becomes the winner. For example, if the statistic is height, the team must quickly line up in order of height from shortest to tallest. When the group is in order by height, team members call out their heights. The first team to finish calling out each person's height in order, wins the round.

If the statistic is age, members line up youngest to oldest. If it's the distance traveled to the reunion, then mileage order is the consideration. A new round begins with a new requirement. Leaders might change each round depending on who has thought up a new way to line up, or the leader might always come from the winning team. This game is a good ice breaker to get the family mixing and having fun together. It can also introduce you to facts about family members.

Game 4: Find Your Family

For "Find Your Family," you need four family groups of at least five members each. (If a family is smaller than five people, add cousins, aunts, or uncles.) A square is created with each family forming a side, and everyone facing the center of the square. But the families don't line up randomly. As in Family Statistics (above), they choose to line up in some order, such as oldest to youngest or birthday order.

In the center of the square is a leader. He or she stands facing one of the lines. Each line member (of all four sides of the square) notes where his or her family is standing in relation to the leader. Each person asks him or herself, "Is the leader facing my line? Does the leader have his or her back to us? Is the leader to our to our right, or to our left?"

The game begins when the leader suddenly spins around facing a new direction. Each line must run and reform in the same order in the same position to the leader as they were before. For example, if a line is behind the leader to begin with, it must reform behind her again in the same order as before. The first team back in correct order yells that it has won.

To make this game more complicated, you can change the family order in relation to the leader, or the order of each line each time the leader spins. This game fosters family cohesiveness, cooperation, and lots of fun and laughter!

Some Family Favorites

A number of families reported having favorite games they play when they get together. Here are some of them.

The Bond Family Game: Killer (or Gotcha!)

Killer is a game listed in *More New Games*. The Bond family of Florida played this game for many years before the book was written. Killer can be played inside or outside and needs at least eight participants in order to be fun. Anyone who can wink and keep a secret can play the game. Some prefer to call this game "Gotcha!" to avoid violent connotations, and possibly scaring younger children.

First, cut up enough little pieces of paper (1" x 1") for the number of people playing. Put an "X" on one piece and leave the others blank. Fold the papers in half twice and put them in a hat or jar from which they can be drawn. Each person draws a piece of paper. The person who receives the X is the Killer and keeps his or her identity a secret from the other players.

The Killer kills by winking at a person. When a person sees someone wink at them, they must pretend to "die," the more melodramatically the better. The killer takes care to wink so no one but the person he or she is winking at sees the wink, because everyone else is out to catch the Killer before getting "killed" by a wink.

When you think you know the identity of the Killer, you can accuse him or her. If you are right, the game is over and you have won. If you are wrong, you are "dead" and out of the game. The Killer tries to kill all other players with a wink without getting caught.

NGF made this game more difficult by requiring the person doing the accusing to be seconded by someone else. Then the two doing the accusing must point in unison at the Killer. If the person they point to is not the Killer, they both die. If they point at two different people, they both die. If they are right, the Killer makes an elaborate confession and the game is over—until the next round.

NGF suggests two variations on this game. One is Killer Marathon in which the game goes on through an entire event (in this case the reunion) with everyone going about their business rather than staying in a group to play. This either could be fun or else make everyone edgy—it depends on your group.

The second version is Killer Plague. In this game, someone dying of a wink can tag another "live" soul and he or she must die, too. So you have to be on the watch, not only for the Killer, but someone dying from a wink. The Bonds report that one of the best players in their family was a six year old with a sly wink who had everyone fooled!

Johnson Family Game: Flashlight Tag

The Johnson cousins of Danville, California, love to play Flashlight Tag, a night time version of Hide and Seek. You need at least four to play this game, each armed with a flashlight. The game is played after dark; the age of the players should be determined by who can stay up after dark and who is not too young to get lost or scared. It is best to designate boundaries for this game because of the dangers of getting lost. Be sure it is a safe area without hidden holes, water, or other dangers. Players should walk through the game area in the daylight so they are familiar with the surroundings. An adult needs to monitor this game and help set the boundaries and time limits.

One person is "It." As in Hide and Seek, the person who is "It" hides his or her eyes and counts to 100 while the others hide, using their flashlights to see where they are going. Two people cannot hide together or in close proximity to each other. If a person hides outside the set game boundary, he or she is automatically "It."

The person who is "It" looks for the other players. When someone is found, "It" tags him or her with a flashlight beam. The players try to make it safely back to base without being tagged by the beam. The first person caught is "It" for the next round. Playing at night adds great suspense to this game and is especially enjoyed by the nine-year-through-teen crowd.

The Johnson elders report having trouble getting the kids to stop playing, so they usually set a quitting time. That way the kids get to bed eventually. Coercing a few willing adults to play seems to make Flashlight Tag even more fun for the kids.

The Havard Family: The Havard Board Game

The Havard family once of Oakland, now of Nevada City, California, have a board game made by one of their sons depicting events in the family's life. The board game has a trail of blocks to follow. Each player throws dice, and reads directions on the block on which their piece falls. (Each playing piece represents a specific member of the family.) The trail leads the family from Oakland to their destination, Nevada City. Funny family events are depicted on each block and on cards that family members draw when landing on certain places. Players are sent forward by some cards or blocks, and back by others.

Anyone can make such a game. Start with an old game board from a thrift store or yard sale. Otherwise, a family artist can draw the game board. Recall funny family events to mark along the trail to the finish. Create game pieces from wood or papier-mache, or use coins.

Adapting Popular Games

A number of families report making their own version of Trivial Pursuit, using family trivia instead of the game's questions. One person makes up the questions ahead of time or has the reunion group submit questions at the reunion. Another variation of a popular game is Family Jeopardy in which information about family members and events must be identified with the correct question. For example, if the answer is "Red bow tie," the question may be "What unusual garment did Uncle John wear to his wedding?"

Create Your Own Games

As you can see, families can be as adept as game companies in coming up with ideas. The examples we've suggested may inspire new games. Or you can stir up your sense of creativity by adapting popular parlor games to the reunion. For instance, do a version of charades that centers around important family events—births, promotions, important trips, relocations, etc. Write these events on pieces of paper, fold them, have someone draw one, and that becomes the theme to be acted out. Obviously, the family game possibilities you can "dream up" are as limitless as your imagination.

There is a commercial board game, *LifeStories*, that we highly recommend for family reunions. Through cards that are drawn, this game gets the participants talking about past events and experiences. The best part is that everyone wins. See p. 213 for more information.

CHAPTER 10

Making History:
Documenting Family Memories

The Art of Interviewing – Two Approaches to Interviewing – Reunions for Genealogical Research – Producing a Family History – Family Directories – Photography – Videos.

Reunions are perfect occasions to gather family history; after all, a family reunion itself is part of your family's history. Common methods of gathering and preserving family history are presented in this chapter.

The Art of Interviewing

Much of a family's history exists only in the memories of the family members. If these memories are not "drawn out" and preserved in some way, they are lost forever as people pass away. To prevent this loss, plan some interviewing and recording sessions to preserve the oral history of your family. *Interviewing* is the means by which these memories are coaxed from people's minds and onto paper or audio/video tape.

However, an interview is only as good as the interviewer. We encourage you to become familiar with this art form and its techniques. We recommend reading *How to Tape Instant Oral Biographies, Recording Your Family History*, or some of the other books mentioned in the Appendix.

To make the most of your interviewing time at the reunion, be well-organized. If the reunion is only one day long, you need to know *exactly* who to talk to and what to ask them. If the reunion lasts several days, create a schedule for each day. To be sure of including certain people, you might make appointments via mail or phone ahead of time. Also, send your potential interviewees a list of questions you intend to ask and facts that you are looking for. Prior knowledge of the questions can help tremendously by giving people a chance to remember or gather the facts and chronology.

Interviews can go off on tangents that might be interesting, but never gather the information you want. On the other hand, tangents can sometimes get you information you never expected. Overall, you should strive for a balance between the "scripted" and the spontaneous.

The traditional method of taking notes is with pencil and paper. However, using tape recorders and video cameras can be most helpful during interviews. Because you can review the answers later, they allow you to concentrate on the interview instead of on note taking.

The tapes can be important additions to a family's archives or they might be used to create a composite tape to share with other members of the family. And videos not only add to the family "scrapbook," they provide a "feature film" to show at the next reunion.

Two Approaches to Interviewing

There are two basic approaches to interviews. One collects oral history; this requires talking directly, one-on-one, with a person—often for hours at a time. A family reunion is not often the best place to do this type of interviewing because of various distractions. For example, an audience may gather, causing self-consciousness. Scheduling "private sessions" a day or two before or after the reunion can help.

The other approach concentrates on collecting facts and figures for charts and family trees. Because "in-depth" interviewing is not required, this way is custom-made for family reunions.

Collecting Oral History. If oral history is your goal, here is a list of questions you can ask during an interview:

1. When and where a person was born, incidents they have been told about their birth.

2. Information about the person's parents: birthplace, where they grew up, schools they attended, professions, physical characteristics, medical history, circumstances of death, where they were buried.

3. Preschool times: memories of siblings, where they lived, life events, medical problems.

4. Childhood memories: where they went to school, their friends, family events, teachers, pets, adventures, vacations, dreams of the future, what life was like, what things had or had not been invented, transportation they used, how far they had to walk to school, cost of common items such as milk, bread, gas, postage stamps, etc.

5. Teenage years: how they felt about growing up, what high school was like, what they did in the summers, how or why they made choices after high school (to work, go to college, get married, or join the military), how they spent their leisure time.

6. Dating and marriage: customs surrounding these events, special friends they didn't marry, how they met their spouse, how they proposed, the wedding, the honeymoon, early marriage, divorce, remarriage, etc.

7. Having children: pregnancy events, where they gave birth, birth circumstances, how children's names were chosen, baptism and blessings, children's personalities, memorable childhood events.

8. Career: jobs they held (what, where and when), salaries, their attitudes about work, what they did, their successes and failures, reasons for occupational changes, how the times affected what they did.

9. Hobbies: how and where they pursued their hobbies, changes in hobbies, any collections and where they are now.

10. Spiritual development: their philosophy of life, beliefs, commitments to ideals, spiritual experiences, psychic events and premonitions, callings they followed, ordinations, promises they made, near death experiences, attitudes and stories about adversity and recovery, attitudes about death and dying, immortality, the meaning of life.

11. Civic activities: involvement in organizations or politics, churches attended, offices held, service to the community, awards won.

12. World view: hopes for future generations, what they still want to accomplish in their lives, attitudes about prosperity and how one gets what they want out of life, their attitudes and feelings during major world events.

13. Medical information: illnesses, diseases, allergies, addictions, causes of death, genetic weaknesses, overcoming terminal illnesses, epidemics, causes for hearing loss or blindness, paralysis, etc.

14. Outstanding people they knew and how their lives were affected, memories of famous people, best friends.

15. How their way of life changed over the years: inventions in their lifetimes, how they traveled and communicated, attitude changes of the young and old, how leisure time was spent, responsibilities of men, women, parents and children, world problems that affected lives, results of world events, times of prosperity, hard times, etc.

16. Family ceremonies and traditions for holidays, religious events, pilgrimages, births and birthdays, marriages, deaths, funerals.

17. Where family items are located: old family homes, graves, diaries, wills, journals, scrapbooks, school annuals, Bibles, homesteads, churches, old family businesses.

18. Family pets, work animals, incidents with animals.

19. Adoptions, second marriages, step- or half-siblings or children, stillborns, childhood deaths.

20. Family recipes and cooking secrets.

After an interview, transcribe it to paper verbatim, even if the grammar is not proper. It can be valuable to other researchers in the "raw" form. Remember that every writer will take a different slant. One writer may like facts; another may try to convey personal philosophy. If you know beforehand what slant you intend to take, develop questions that will elicit the information you need.

Collecting Facts. If you want to collect facts—names, dates, places—at the reunion, announce in one of the mailers what you are looking for and what kinds of things people can bring to help you. Ask for old Bibles, journals, wills, letters, birth and death certificates, newspaper clippings, old genealogies, church records, old photos, military records, naturalization papers, marriage certificates. At the reunion, collect these items in a central location where researchers can view them. Perhaps someone in the family can bring a portable photocopier.

If you must rely on the memory of those present for facts, create lists of what you need, question those who might know, record what you find out and, most important, document your sources. If the reunion is so large that you cannot personally interview everyone who has information you want, make a fact-gathering chart that people can fill in at their leisure.

Medical History. The Crom family had a *medical chart* available at their reunion. They were interested in certain types of medical problems that seemed to be cropping up in the younger generation. They listed these medical problems down the side of the chart and asked people to fill in the names, dates, and addresses of others in the family who suffered from these ailments. Helpful pamphlets are available from the March of Dimes to aid you in collecting medical information from your family. See the Appendix and Figure 21.

FIGURE 21. Checking over the medical history charts.

Reunions for Genealogical Research

Some reunions are held specifically to do genealogical research. The family of Helen Hardin Hoots has such reunions.
She reports that the "most memorable part [of the reunion]
was meeting correspondents....and learning of their work and
ancestral research." If your reunion is for this purpose, careful
planning will help researchers achieve their goals. Query the
researchers ahead of time to determine what they would like to
accomplish at the reunion; set up the schedule based on these
needs. This may mean scheduling library time, interviewing
time, touring time, etc. However, your plans should be flexible;
for instance, if people doing research in the library don't want
to quit, they should be able to continue there as long as they
want. But constant study and research can be tiring, too. Plan
some rest and recreation to give people a break and the opportunity to visit.

Producing a Family History

A family history is the story of your ancestors, but can also
include living relatives. What better way to present special
family qualities and philosophies than by preparing the story
of the past in an easy-to-read form. A well-written, well-
researched family history can be as exciting to read as a good

biography. However, unless enthusiastic-yet-careful writing and editing are done, family histories can be rather boring, fac-

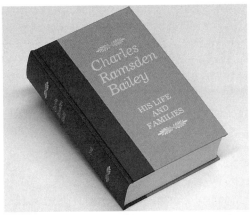

tual accounts of family chronology. But don't be discouraged if you aren't a great writer—get the facts down anyway. A great writer may come along later or funds may someday be available for professional assistance.

FIG 22. Specialized companies can produce your family history. Photo courtesy Family History Publishers; see address in Appendix.

Often family histories have little genealogical value due to an abundance of erroneous facts, such as dates, places, names, and relationships. If you write a family history, use the best documented sources you can find; however, check these sources against others, and have a person familiar with the family proofread to look for factual errors. Your family proofreader may remember dates and events differently. Rather than having such discrepancies lead to disagreements, use this information to research more extensively.

Then have someone *unfamiliar* with your history read over the preliminary drafts and make suggestions. Often events you portray are so familiar to you that you are unaware of the lack of clarity.

No "fact" is assumed correct in genealogical research until it is verified a number of different ways. There is much room for error, especially if you are relying on people's memories. Even printed materials such as newspaper articles can be erroneous. One woman reported finding nine errors in her mother's obituary! If you feel that facts in your sources, or in your history, may not be totally correct, communicate this to the reader. Document your sources in a bibliography; future generations will be grateful and you won't be adding to the world of misinformation.

Problems with grammar, punctuation, syntax, and spelling may also be encountered. If you are using a computer, get a spelling checker. Have a proofreader who is a good speller and grammarian help polish your final draft. There are a number of good style manuals which clarify grammar, punctuation, and word usage: *The Chicago Manual of Style, The Gregg Reference Manual,* and *Publication Manual of the American Psychological Association* are just a few.

A desktop publishing system can be used for creating family histories. All aspects of book design can be handled by the software including line spacing, type styles, headings, page numbering, etc. (This book is a good example.) The cost depends on how much work you do yourself. Compiling, writing, and editing are the most expensive elements. If your family can do these things, a 300-page hard cover book can be produced for around $10–30 per book, depending on the quantity printed. Also see "Desktop Publishing," p. 185.

There are many books available on the subjects of self-publishing, printing, book design, writing and editing, how to copyright your work, and anything else you need to know to produce a high quality family history. For more information, read some of the books mentioned in the Appendix.

A tip: Including color photos in a book is very expensive, especially if you print a small number of books. Pasting color photographs into your book by hand is an inexpensive alternative to color printing. Since photocopy machines have fairly decent color reproduction abilities these days, color photocopies could be pasted in instead of photos.

To keep histories up to date, print them in numbered volumes. This also allows you to concentrate on one period of time rather than facing the overwhelming task of covering three or four centuries in one work. Any time period can be chosen; volumes can cover one or two generations, one century, or just fifty years. Another advantage of producing one volume at a time is that the work and costs are spread over a longer time period. Also, smaller volumes at a lower price will be easier to sell (if that's how you finance the project) than one huge volume.

If your family history is carefully researched and of high quality, you may be able to sell it commercially. Genealogy libraries, specialized book dealers, and genealogy societies are the usual buyers. See the Appendix for more information.

Family Directories

As the title implies, a *family directory* is a directory or reference book of family-related information, usually published annually. Family directories differ from newsletters in that they contain addresses, facts, dates, lists, and not much news. For example they might list births, deaths, marriages, graduations, anniversaries, people serving in the military, family association officers and committees, as well as the current mailing list. The size is usually $8\frac{1}{2}$ x $5\frac{1}{2}$. Directory costs can be covered by membership dues, or they can be sold, either as a money maker or just to break even.

Family associations may use the directory as their annual report including, beside the items above, the year-end financial statement, and the minutes of the board meeting(s). The directory is usually mailed at the end of the association's fiscal year; however, a November mailing brings the most recent mailing list to the members before holiday cards are addressed. The association's constitution and bylaws can also be printed, along with its goals and purposes.

Most directories can be produced following the steps used to create newsletters (see Chapter 14). However, you will want a more durable cover on a directory; it may be referred to many times during the year. Most printers and copy shops carry card stock paper that makes a substantial cover, and comes in a range of colors and textures. It's helpful to print a different color cover each year to avoid confusing one issue with another.

It's critical that a directory be proofread at least twice before printing. With so many details—addresses, phone numbers, names, and zip codes—it's easy to transpose numbers, forget a middle initial, or leave out a "Jr." in a name. Carefully proofread anything produced by a typesetter as well. Typesetting looks more official, but there still may be errors.

Photography

Be sure that *some* type of photographic or videographic documentation takes place at your reunion. At the very least, maintain a scrapbook of candid reunion photos. If necessary, hire a professional to take these photos. An "on-going" scrapbook will become valuable and add interest to future reunions.

Group photos are the most common photos taken at family reunions. If indoors, they should be taken by a professional because indoor settings present lighting problems few amateurs can overcome. Most pros don't like to take group photos of more than about 80 people. More than that and the faces in the photo become indistinct. A larger format photo, say 11 x 18, can be a solution to this problem. Of course, it will cost more.

One difficulty in setting up a group photo is to keep faces from being hidden behind other faces. People think if they can see the camera, then their entire face will appear in the photo; this isn't necessarily the case. It takes a lot of time and an experienced photographer to arrange everyone properly so all faces show. For large groups, figure at least 30–40 minutes for set-up, and warn the group ahead of time so they don't get disgruntled during the wait.

An 8 x 10 color print should cost between $9 and $15 each (1992), depending on quantity. It's best to include the cost of the photo in the registration fee, rather than charge separately for it. Be sure to offer the photo to those who can't attend. Have a special place on the registration form for this, and don't forget to add the mailing cost to the price.

An experienced amateur photographer with good equipment can usually take a decent outdoor group photo. With a tripod and camera with a timer, the photographer can also get in the picture. Be sure to schedule the photo session *well before* anyone has departed for home. Many groups miss the opportunity to get everyone in the picture by not scheduling it early enough.

A big problem at family reunions is disorganization at photography sessions. It's helpful to plan ahead. Find a site that will hold everyone, and where the lighting is proper at the time of day when the photo session is scheduled. Set up the camera on a tripod *beforehand* to see how wide a group can be photographed. If it's helpful, set out side markers to indicate the maximum width.

If you meet at a site that has particular meaning to your family, you may want to photograph the location. Homes built by ancestors, tombstones in a family cemetery, the church that your family helped build, the college your mom attended, the old family business, Uncle Joe's collection of antique cars, etc., are all important. You can include an interview of a person who remembers the most about each special place.

The Fun of Videos

Videotapes of reunions are becoming increasingly popular as video recording and playback equipment becomes cheaper and of higher quality. Nearly 80% of American households own VCR's, and that percentage will only increase over the next few years. Of course, you do not need to own a VCR to enjoy a reunion video. The machines are extremely inexpensive to rent for one evening; all you need is a TV.

Video cameras are getting easier to use, and as a result, amateur videography is getting better. If someone in your family is bringing a video camera anyway, this may eliminate the need for a professional. There are duplicating services that can make copies of the original video for other family members to purchase. In your mailers, ask who will be bringing video cameras and if they would be willing to make copies for others. However, a professional will almost always do a better job. Their equipment is usually of better quality, they know how to minimize "camera shake," they can edit, add captions and background music, etc. In some cases, "shots" of old photos and memorabilia, even old movies, can be added. The difference, of course, is cost.

Some professionals charge a base fee plus so much per copy sold; others do not charge a base fee, but must be guaranteed a minimum purchase. In the latter case, the committee or the company advertises the tape through the mail beforehand. If not enough videos are pre-sold, then the service is cancelled or a higher price is negotiated.

Reunion videos usually contain two types of live footage. One is the "interview" where each person is asked questions to which he or she replies on camera. The other concentrates on "candid shots." The camera operator wanders through the reunion taking footage of people talking, playing, eating, etc.

Whatever you do, make sure that everyone present—from the youngest to the oldest—is on the tape *somewhere*. The biggest disadvantage of using a professional is their lack of familiarity with the family. Assign a "helper" from the family to assist the camera person. This assistant should have a list of all attendees and check off people as they are videotaped. Be sure to include special performances and set up interviews with key people.

If you hire a professional and your reunion is two or three days long, you can save money by videotaping during one day only. Schedule important events for this day.

A large reunion group may be able to find a professional willing to videotape on a completely freelance basis. There is no charge to the reunion committee, and the sale of the product is done through the mail by the video company several weeks after the reunion. However, an arrangement of this kind often involves beginners who are trying to break into the field. This doesn't necessarily mean that quality will be compromised, but it *does* mean that you should be careful. Even though the video service is not costing you anything, your group will expect a high quality product, and you are the one in charge of selecting the videographer. The quality of a videotape depends on the skill of the person operating the camera, the skill of the editor, and the skill of the interviewer. For low-budget assignments, this may be the same person. It's very important to preview a reunion video that the company has already produced. Then call someone on that reunion committee to find out how they liked the video and what they thought about dealing with the company.

CHAPTER 11

Distinctive Destinations:
Reunions They'll Never Forget

*Luxury Resorts – Shipboard Reunions – Enjoying History –
In Search of Your Roots – The Great Outdoors – Ecotourism –
Cowboy Adventures – Native American Adventures.*

Most family reunions are held in backyards, neighborhood parks, local community centers, or banquet rooms of nearby hotels or motels.

But what about those *special reunions*—the ones that celebrate a special event, investigate a special interest, answer a special concern, or fulfill a special wish? For instance, a reunion might honor the day that Grandma Sophia immigrated to this country from Naples. Or a reunion might explore a family's interest in Native Americans and how they live.

Another reunion might address environmental concerns and involve tidying up a forest preserve. Yet another reunion might find family members fulfilling a long-held dream of vacationing at a luxurious resort. These reunions deserve (sometimes require) special surroundings—distinctive, off-the-beaten-path sites and activities.

To stir up your imagination and get the creative juices flowing, this chapter suggests a variety of places to go and things to do. However, some of these suggestions might seem rather expensive. Whenever possible, off-season rates and group reductions are mentioned. Please bear in mind these sites are not suggested as candidates for yearly reunions; rather, for very special, once-in-a-decade or lifetime events. Fund-raising efforts of several "regular" reunions might be directed towards financing a special reunion the family will never forget.

A wonderful source of ideas is *Super Family Vacations: Resort and Adventure Guide* by Martha Shirk and Nancy Klepper, revised edition, HarperCollins, New York.

Luxury Resorts: Living the Good Life for Less

You'll usually find luxury resorts clustered around tourist areas. Three good examples are San Diego, Orlando and Scottsdale (a resort community near Phoenix). While these resorts are often destinations in themselves—offering a wide choice of recreational activities and a variety of dining options—they also have the added advantage of being near world-class sightseeing attractions. Sea World and the famous zoo are located in San Diego, Disney World in Orlando, and Scottsdale is surrounded by cowboy ranches and Native American reservations as well as being a few hours' drive from the Grand Canyon.

During the busy seasons, these luxury resorts can be quite pricey. However, it's an entirely different story during their respective off-seasons. For instance, as Scottsdale's temperatures soar from Memorial Day through Labor Day, rates at the resorts can drop by as much as 70–75 percent.

In addition to attractive rates, these resorts provide luxurious accommodations as well as ample meeting and banquet space. And the children/teen programs offered by some should be of special interest to those planning family reunions. After all, keeping the youngsters occupied and entertained is often the key to a successful reunion.

These children's programs might include visiting a petting zoo, decorating a T-shirt, or enjoying a nature tour. Teens could join a jeep rally or a horseback ride in the desert, complete with cowboy guides. Tennis and golf clinics are specially designed for the younger player's needs—with plenty of attention from the resident pros. These special activities are offered during holidays, weekends, and daily throughout the summer.

Two Scottsdale resorts offer superlative children/teen programs as well as reduced summer rates. At the Hyatt Regency Scottsdale you'll find "Camp Hyatt Kachina" designed for ages 3–12. "Kamp Kachina" is the prototype for Camp Hyatt, which has been implemented in many Hyatt hotels and resorts throughout the country. "Rock Hyatt" is the teen program. For information and reservations, call 800/233-1234, or write: 7500 E. Doubletree Ranch Rd., Scottsdale, AZ 85258.

Also located in Scottsdale, The Phoenician Resort provides outstanding children/teen programs. The "Funician Club for Children" is a daily, supervised program for kids 5–12. Each day of the week, the program features a different theme, with activities to match. For information and reservations, call 800/888-8234, or write: 6000 E. Camelback Rd., Scottsdale, AZ 85251.

Some destination resorts are literally "off the beaten path"—up in the mountains or off by a beach. While they may not offer proximity to sightseeing attractions, they do offer a lot of peace and quiet, and natural beauty—exactly what some family reunion planners are looking for!

At Mountain Laurel Resort in Pennsylvania's Pocono Mountains, you'll find a great ambiance, ample meeting space, and an extensive children's program. Initiated more than a decade ago, the resort's "Leave the Kids with Us" program for youngsters five years and under has been expanded into "Kidtracks Krew" for children six years and over. The junior program operates year around; the "graduate program" is of-

FIGURE 23. Clockwise from top left: Tug-of-war at Rock Hyatt; building sandcastles and cooking classes at Camp Hyatt; miniature golf and storytelling at Mountain Laurel Resort; water slide at the Phoenician Resort.

fered on weekends, holidays, and daily during the summer. Staged both indoors and outdoors, activities include creek stomping, nature hikes, sports tournaments, swimming instruction, treasure hunts, horse-drawn hay/sleigh rides, magic shows, crafts and special seasonal events. Best of all, the Mountain Laurel Resort offers their complete child care and activity program for a one-time fee of $10 to cover the cost of each child's T-shirt. For information and reservations, call 717/443-8411, or write: PO Box 126, White Haven, PA 18661.

Shipboard Family Reunions

There are people who need the deck of a ship underfoot and a sail snapping in the wind to feel that they've "gotten away from it all." If the members of your group like to be surrounded with H_2O, consider a water-oriented family reunion.

Of course, bear in mind that there are all kinds of sailors. Some prefer the pampered life aboard a cruise ship or yacht as opposed to hauling up sail on a windjammer. Others might seek the "homey" atmosphere of a houseboat. To show the variety available, we'll discuss several options: cruise ships, steamboats, windjammers, and houseboats.

A great source for water-oriented reunion ideas is Michael White's *Floating Vacations* (see the Appendix). This book lists 203 houseboat rental companies throughout the U.S. and Canada and covers white-water rafting, canoeing, and yachting as well as houseboating.

Cruise Ships

Wouldn't it be wonderful to be waited on hand and foot, served gourmet-style meals and snacks several times a day, party every night, explore ports-of-call, and not have to worry about the kids having a good time?

Welcome aboard Carnival Lines! Offering three- or four-day mini-vacations, Carnival has three ships—*Mardi Gras, Carnival* and *Fantasy*—sailing to the Bahamas from either Port Canaveral or Miami. Aside from all the attentive service, the line's year-round supervised children's activities, "Camp Carnival," make these trips especially attractive to family reunions.

How much will all this cost? Maybe less than you think. When shopping for a cruise via a travel agency or a cruise company, remember that the prices cited in the brochures aren't cast in stone. In most instances, they represent "high hopes" on the part of the cruise lines. Price cutting is pretty much the norm. While cruise companies cut their rates like the airlines, unlike the airlines, they often don't advertise the reductions. And they don't offer the same rates to every travel agency. So the name of the game is shop around! (For a list of travel agents in your area who specialize in cruises, send a stamped, self-addressed envelope to The National Association of Cruise Only Agencies, P.O. Box 7209, Freeport, NY 11520). And don't hestitate to deal directly with the cruise company, especially if you have a large group.

Note: Be aware that round-trip transportation to the cruise line pier from hotel or airport can add up to $50 or more.

Steamboats

For adults and children alike, there's nothing like the excitement of a steamboat coming into view, calliope playing, paddle wheel churning. Representing an important part of the American Heritage, a steamboat provides a marvelous setting for a family reunion.

The Steamboatin' Lines famous *Delta Queen* and *Mississippi Queen* embark from a number of cities: Minneapolis/St. Paul, Pittsburgh, Cincinnati, Louisville, St. Louis, Nashville, Chattanooga, Memphis, and New Orleans. While a dizzying number of themes and options are available, the "In the Good Old Summertime" vacations are described as the perfect setting for a family reunion.

Staged in different areas of the country, this "summertime" steamboat trip can range from 3–7 days. Minimum group size is 10 full-fare passengers and discounts can add up to 40%. If you want to discuss discount fares with the company, call 800/458-6789, or write: Delta Queen Steamboat Co., Robin Street Wharf, New Orleans, LA 70130-1890.

Windjammers

Family reunion groups who must "go down to the sea in ships" may opt for a half-week (or full week) sail off the beauti-

FIGURE 24. Clockwise from top left: Windjamming off the Maine Coast; aboard a windjammer; paddle wheeler Delta Queen; houseboating on Lake Powell; ice cream party on a Carnival Line cruise ship; the Grand Saloon on the steamboat Mississippi Queen.

ful Maine Coast. Here there are no phones, no TVs, no newspapers, and no engine noise—just wonderful scenery, a sense of adventure, the feeling of history, the warmth of camaraderie and absolutely no pressure. However, there is plenty to do—help the crew haul up sails, swim, fish, take photos, and join in spontaneous races with other vessels.

Accommodating up to 44 passengers, a sea-going windjammer is a great way for family members to get to know one another without outside attractions and distractions. The season is Memorial Day to Labor Day (give or take a little), with the peak season in July and August. Rates are lower in June and September. For more information, call the Maine Windjammer Association at 800/624-6380, or write: PO Box 317, Rockport, ME 04856.

The age limit for "general" cruises is usually 15 and up. However, if you rent the entire boat (capacities vary between 20 and 44, minimum of 3 days), then the boat is "yours," and any age is permissible. One company with such an arrangement is Maine Windjammer Cruises (capacity of their boat is 29). For more information, call them at 207/236-2938, or write: PO Box 617, Camden, ME 04843.

Houseboats

How about a houseboat reunion? Piloting a houseboat is easier than driving a car and you don't need a special license. Lake Powell, the dramatic centerpiece of the Utah/Arizona area which includes Monument Valley, the Grand Canyon, and Zion National Park, is one of the centers of houseboat activity in the U.S. With 2000 miles of shoreline, 2 lodges, 4 full-time marinas, a 9-hole golf course, plus tennis, hiking, bicycling, dam and museum tours, Lake Powell is truly a reunion planner's paradise. Their houseboats come in three sizes, each with creature comforts that include a bathroom with hot shower, refrigerator/freezer, fully-equipped kitchen with stove, etc. Seasonal pricing and packages can offer substanial savings on both lodging and boat rentals. For more information, call 800/528-6154 or 602/484-9090, or write: Lake Powell Resorts and Marinas, 2916 N. 35th Ave. #8, Phoenix, AZ 85017. Minimum rental for houseboats during summer season (May 17th through October 15th) is three days.

Note: Many places offer off-season and/or group discounts. However, these reductions depend upon availability. For smooth sailing, reservation-wise, it's important to act early. For a list of houseboat rental agencies, see Houseboat Association of America in the Appendix.

Enjoying History: Past, Present, and Yours

Historical sites provide fascinating settings for groups interested in this country's heritage as well as in their own. Involvement in such a family reunion can be on two levels: as a spectactor enjoying history or as a participant enjoying history brought to life. The examples we give here—Colonial Williamsburg, Grand Canyon Railway, and Living History Farms—make both levels possible.

Colonial Williamsburg

Located midway between Norfolk and Richmond, Williamsburg is the re-creation of an 18th century Virgina community and is America's premier historical resort. Brought to life with busy shops, horse-drawn carriages, and costumed characters, Williamsburg consists of 88 original structures—homes, businesses, public buildings—that have been restored and preserved.

Reunion members can experience Colonial Williamsburgs's past by visiting museums, shops, mansions, and slave quarters to see how men, women, and children of that time lived, worked and played. The site can be enjoyed as "history brought to life" by taking part in various activities. Discover how people traveled two centuries ago with the Stage Wagon Tour. Explore the life-styles of African-Americans with the Other Half Tour. Join 18th century dancing and lawn games; learn how to make ornaments from that time period.

Special children's activities are offered throughout the year at various times. These include ox cart rides, fife and drum presentations, tours and magic shows. Special programs are available for children 4–12 at a nominal cost.

Lodging options can be contemporary or colonial. Ideally located between the Historic Area and Visitor's Center, the Governor's Inn is recommended for families. Reduced packages

FIGURE 25. Clockwise from top left: Scene at Colonial Williamsburg; Grand Canyon Railway; hombres set to hold up the train; three scenes from Living History Farms.

are available during the off-season. Groups of more than 15 receive discounts. For more information, call 800-HISTORY, or write: PO Box C, Williamsburg, VA 23187.

Note: In addition to Williamsburg lodging, a wide range of nearby hotels and motels offer other options.

Grand Canyon Railway

Located in Williams, Arizona, less than 3 hours from Phoenix, the Grand Canyon Railway Depot offers a preview of the exciting trip to and from the Grand Canyon. As the 1910 steam locomotive pulls up and passengers get ready to board, a mock shoot-out between the marshall and some "varmints" takes place. Despite all the hullabaloo, the train pulls out at precisely 9:30 a.m. and everyone is on their way in the comfort of authentically restored 1920's Harriman coach cars.

During the leisurely $2\frac{1}{2}$ hour trip, passengers are entertained by beautiful vistas, wildlife sightings, and live music provided by banjo and guitar players. Stepping off the train at the Grand Canyon Depot—the last log depot in the United States—everyone has plenty of time to take a bus or air tour, go sightseeing, visit the museums and stores, or hike around the majestic South Rim. On the return trip, there's great excitement again when the train is "held up" by some bad hombres who come riding in on horseback. However, the marshall comes to the rescue, peace is restored, and the passengers arrive back in Williams safely.

While everyone enjoys the Grand Canyon Steam Railroad, railroad buffs think they've died and gone to heaven. As a family reunion site, it uniquely combines a historical trip with a visit to one of the world's greatest sights. (It should be noted that parking has become difficult at the Grand Canyon, especially during the summer.) Large reunions (90 or multiples of 90) can have their own railroad cars, thus ensuring greater privacy and enjoyment. Groups of 30 or more receive a discount. For more information, call 800/843-8723 or 800/843-8724, or write: 518 E. Bill Williams Ave., Williams, AZ 86046.

Note: Daily service runs June through September. October through May, the schedule is reduced.

Living History Farms

Located in Urbandale, Iowa (10 miles from downtown Des Moines), Living History Farms is a 600-acre, open-air museum that re-creates the history of agriculture in the Midwest. The buildings, planting methods, and livestock are authentic from the time periods represented. Interpreters dressed in historic clothing re-enact the daily routines of early Iowans and help visitors appreciate the artistry of the craftsmen who founded the state's first town. Walking trails connect the 1700 Ioway Native American village, the 1850 Pioneer and 1900 Farms, and as in Colonial Williamsburg, Living History Farms can be enjoyed by seeing how these settlers and Natives Americans lived and worked in the past. By joining the numerous activities scheduled through the summer, reunion members can experience the "living history" of the farm on another level. For instance, during the summer, games include leap frog, greased pole climbing, sack races, pig calling, and foot races. (If this is a little "too active" for older members, they might try square dancing!)

Summer day-camp sessions are available on a weekly basis for children entering grades 3–6 in the fall. Group accommodations and discounts for 20 or more are available. For more information, call 515/278-5286, or write: 2600 NW 111 St., Urbandale, IA 50322.

In Search of Your Roots

With the publication of Alex Haley's *Roots* in 1976, both African-American and families of other origins developed a greater interest in their respective histories. As a result, Mr. Haley was a driving force behind the continued growing popularity of organized family reunions.

With the current emphasis on ethnic origins and pride, this interest is destined to become even more intense. In ethnic family reunions, the trend is dramatized by the record numbers of African-Americans seeking their past in the South. Among the most popular destinations visited by both individual families and groups are The Black Heritage Tour in Natchez, Mississippi (800/647-6724, PO Box 1485, Natchez, MS 39121-1485), and the birth home of Dr. Martin Luther King,

Jr., in Atlanta, Georgia (404/331-3920, 522 Auburn Ave., Atlanta, GA 30312).

There are many ways for ethnic groups to celebrate their heritage and history in a family reunion setting. For instance, if Grandma Lucy immigrated on March 3rd from Yugoslavia, you might consider staging a family reunion back in Yugoslavia on that same day. Group air fares could lower the cost considerably. Aside from being the "thrill of a lifetime" for Grandma, it would be a wonderful opportunity to catch up with some "long-lost" relatives, not to mention genealogy.

Of course, you don't have to visit the "old country" to stage a history-oriented family reunion. Why not consider one with an educational twist? During the summer, the Smithsonian Institution in Washington DC, offers their "Campus on the Mall." Among one-weekend classes offered are subjects that might appeal to some ethnic groups such as "A Pilgrimage to China" and "Classic Arab Folk Tales." Since Washington DC is very much geared to touring families, your group could stay at a nearby hotel (enjoying group rates) and conduct any group meetings in a conference room. For more information on classes, call The Smithsonian at 202/357-3030, or write: 1100 Jefferson Dr. #3077, Washington, DC 20560. For information on accommodations, call the District of Columbia Visitor's Bureau at 202/789-7000, or write: 1212 New York Ave. NW #600, Washington, DC 20005.

The Great Outdoors: Back to Nature

For some of us, a family reunion spent "getting back to Nature" might be a picnic in a city park. However, with all the lakes, rivers, mountains, wildernesses, and other open spaces available, it's a shame not to move to a more exciting setting. Members of your group could be spectactors, such as bison or bird watchers. Or they could be participants in a hike or cattle drive. Or both. Depending on the group size, ages, and attitudes, you might want to "rough it" in tents pitched under the stars. On the other hand, group members might prefer to stay in a spacious lodge with comfortable private rooms and maid service. The choices are seemingly endless. *Camping in the National Park System* and *The National Park System Index*

are good sources of information. These books should be available in most libraries.

Montecito-Sequoia Lodge

You can't beat Montecito-Sequoia Lodge for that real mountain feeling. Located at 7500' in California's Sierra Nevada Mountains, it has an unsurpassed view of 13,000' peaks and is near to Sequoia National Park, Kings Canyon National Park, and the giant sequoia "big trees." Program and activity directors are always available and many activities are scheduled daily with never a lack of things to do. Summer activities include water skiing, rifelry, archery, fencing, trampoline, tennis, volleyball, horseback riding, swimming, canoeing, paddle boating, naturalist hikes, campfire/group singing, ping pong, horseshoes, arts and crafts, theme nights, family variety shows and more. Call 800/227-9900 or write the main office at 1485 Redwood Dr, Los Altos, CA 94024. Capacity: 175.

YMCA of the Rockies

To the best of our knowledge, the YMCA of the Rockies hosts more family reunions than any other facility in the world —over 600 per year. There are actually two facilities, Estes Park Center and Snow Mountain Ranch. Located 65 miles northwest of Denver, Estes Park Center offers affordable accommodations of all kinds, and provides nearly 40 meeting rooms on the 860-acre property. Popular for family reunions is the Pattie Hyde Barclay Reunion Lodge, with a capacity of 72.

Located 80 miles west of Denver, the 4900-acre Snow Mountain Ranch enfolds forests of pine and fir as well as cozy cabins, spacious lodges, and numerous meeting facilities. Accommodating meetings from 20 to 1300, the ranch has 5 family reunion cabins (capacity: 25 each) with sweeping views of the surrounding wilderness. Both the Center and the Ranch offer numerous recreational activities, from swimming to skiing, nature hikes to crafts. Call 800/777-YMCA, or write: YMCA of the Rockies, Estes Park, CO 80511-2800.

FIGURE 26. Clockwise from top left: Family reunion, sail boating at Montecito-Sequoia Lodge; family reunion, nordic skiing at Snow Mountain Ranch; hayride, group hike at Estes Park Center.

Glorieta Conference Center/Ridgecrest Conference Center

Glorieta Conference Center in New Mexico, and its sister property, Ridgecrest in North Carolina are two of the best facilities for family reunions in the U.S. Owned and operated by the Sunday School Board of the Southern Baptist Convention, both sites rival the YMCA of the Rockies (previous page) in activities, prices, scenery and safe, Christian environment. Glorieta is situated 18 miles east of Santa Fe right on I-25; Ridgecrest is 17 miles east of Asheville. Activities at both facilities include volleyball, basketball, softball, tennis, ping pong, badminton, frisbee, horseshoes, billiards, miniature golf and white water rafting nearby. Accommodations are available with or without kitchen facilities. Glorieta Conference Center, PO Box 8, Glorieta, NM 87535, 800/797-4222. Ridgecrest Conference Center, PO Box 128, Ridgecrest, NC 28770, 704/669-8022.

FIGURE 26a. Activities at Glorieta (left); kids having a good time at Ridgecrest.

Ecotourism

With environmental concern being an international issue, it is not surprising that ecotourism is becoming more popular. Combining a sense of adventure with an appreciation of Nature, it can offer many variations: mountain climbing treks, archaeological explorations, field trips, etc. Whatever variation you choose, ecotourism can be a rewarding theme for family reunions.

While more and more travel agencies are gearing up for

FIGURE 27.   Clockwise from top left: An arrowhead making demonstration at the Archaeological Conservancy; checking things out with telescope and binoculars at The Nature Place; mother/daughter and father/son teams during Family Week at Crow Canyon Archaeological Center; making Anasazi-style pots during the same Family Week.

ecotourism, it's great fun to plan your own environmentally oriented family reunion. The following examples may stimulate your thinking. For other ideas, contact groups such as The National Audubon Society, 613 Riversfill Rd, Greenwich, CT 06831, 203/869-2017; Maine Photographic Workshops, 2 Central St, Rockport, ME 04856, 207/236-8581; Smithsonian Study Tours & Seminars, 1100 Jefferson Dr. SW, Room 3045, MRC 702, Washington, DC 20560, 202/357-4700.

The Nature Place

Located 35 miles west of Colorado Springs, Colorado, The Nature Place welcomes family reunions to a quiet, relaxed year-round mountain retreat. Designated by the National Park Service as a "National Environmental Study Area," the 6000 acre center offers numerous programs, including astronomy, botany, geology, ornithology, and wildlife observation. Lodge and studio apartments constructed of natural wood, native rock, and large expanses of glass can accommodate up to 100. Conference facilities are available. A deluxe sports complex contains a pool, jacuzzi, sauna, and exercise room; tennis and volleyball courts are outside. For more information, call 719/748-3475 or 719/748-3341, or write: Colorado Outdoor Education Center, Florissant, CO 80816.

The Archaeological Conservancy

Wildlife, oceans and rivers, forests and mountains aren't the only parts of the environment being threatened. Each day, archaelogical ruins are being lost forever, along with the invaluable historical information they possess. The Archaeological Conservancy is a national nonprofit organization dedicated to acquiring and permanently preserving the nation's best sites. It's holdings range from Ohio to New Mexico, Michigan to California. As part of their educational effort, this group stages numerous trips to important archaeological centers, such as Mesa Verde National Park in Colorado, Ohio's Hopewell Complex, and the Sonoran Desert of southern Arizona and northern Mexico. Recreational adventures are available as well. A rafting trip down the San Juan River in southern Utah is offered twice a year, June and September. Membership is necessary. For more information call 505/266-1540, or write: The Archealogical Conservancy, 5301 Central Ave NE, Albuquerque, NM 87108.

Crow Canyon Archaeological Center

Located 4 miles from Cortez, Colorado, and 10 miles from the entrance to Mesa Verde National Park, Crow Canyon Archaeological Center is a nonprofit organization dedicated to archaeological research and education. The archaeologists there have been carefully piecing together information that will help us understand the prehistoric people who once flourished in this area. Open to all age groups, the center offers participants a unique opportunity to combine meaningful research with hands-on experience. Shared accommodations are available in picturesque log hogans or in the Crow Canyon Lodge.

The special Family Week Program in August allows family members to share the excitement of a "dig"! Open to parents or grandparents and children in the 4th grade or higher, the program has students in grades 4 through 6 excavate in a simulated dig and participate in a simulated lab. Junior high students excavate with adults in the field on a half-day basis. High school students join adults in the standard Adult Research Program. Also open to families are the day programs where participants examine artifacts, attempt to reconstruct lifeways, tour a lab, and visit a working archaeological site. For more information call 800/422-8975, or write: 23390 County Road K, Cortez, CO 81321.

Cowboy Adventures

You wake up to the sound of horses whinneying and cattle bellowing; the smell of coffee boiling on the stove. You gallop along the banks of a cottonwood-lined creek. Hunker down with wranglers by a campfire with some fresh-from-the-stream trout for dinner. More and more people are discovering the fun and excitement shared by those "dudes" in *City Slickers*. With a little research and some advance planning, your group can experience a family reunion they'll be spinning yarns about for years!

A great resource for "scouting" a cowboy-style family

FIGURE 28. Clockwise from top left: Lunch by the water, trailriding at The Alisal Guest Ranch, Solvang, CA; chuckwagon grub at Dixie Dude Ranch, Bandera, TX; a wagon train excursion near El Dorado, KS; Children dress up at a Native American powwow in Flagstaff, AZ.

reunion is Eugene Kilgore's *Ranch Vacations,* John Muir Publications, 800/888-7504. This book covers dude/guest ranches, cross-country skiing ranches, and fly-fishing ranches.

The Alisal Guest Ranch

Located 35 miles northwest of Santa Barbara on a 10,000 acre working cattle ranch secluded in the Santa Ynez Valley, The Alisal is California's only full-service guest ranch. For half a century, the same families have returned year after year and The Alisal is now hosting the 4th generation. The Ranch features 73 cottage studios and suites, all with wood-burning fireplaces and refrigerators, two championship golf courses, 7 tennis courts, many kinds of horseback activities, a swimming pool, a 90-acre lake for fishing and water sports, and a year-round children's program. The Alisal Guest Ranch, 1054 Alisal Rd, Solvang, CA 93463, 800/425-4725.

The Dixie Dude Ranch

Don't go callin' this a resort ranch. The Dixie Dude is a 725-acre old-time working stock ranch founded in 1901. But of course you don't have to do any work at all. Just take it easy and have a good time with your family. Activities include horseback riding, hayrides, campfire sing-alongs, dancing, hiking, arrowhead hunting and barbeques. Located in the Texas Hill Country; 55 miles northwest of San Antonio. Airport pickup is available with prior arrangement. Dixie Dude Ranch, PO Box 548, Bandera, TX 78003, 800/375-Y'ALL.

Wagon Trains

For more than a decade, a Kansas company has offered "weekend pioneers" the opportunity to relive the adventures of their forefathers, enjoy the scenic beauty of the famous Flint Hills area, partake of chuckwagon meals over an open fire, and sleep out under the stars. Wagon train trips are overnight, returning to the point of embarkation the next day. Excursions are scheduled from the middle of June to the middle of September. Group rates are available. For more information, call 316/321-6300, or write: Overland Wagon Train Trips, Box 1076, El Dorado, KS 67042. Space is limited. Reserve early!

Native American Adventures

With the advent of films such as *Dances with Wolves*, there's more and more interest in "the people who discovered Columbus."

Both the United States and Canada are home to dozens of tribes (they prefer to be called nations) and reservations. In Arizona alone, there are 15 nations and 20 reservations. Each nation's culture, traditions, features, languages, and size differ considerably. There are geographical distinctions as well; for example, the Hopi live on "top of the world" on the high mesas in north-central Arizona, and the Havasupai live within the depths of the Grand Canyon.

With growing interest in Native Americans becoming evident, some nations and reservations are becoming more tourist oriented. Many have camping and RV facilities; others have hotels, arts and crafts centers, even water sports arenas.

Some Native American centers are setting up travel agencies; for example, the Native American Travel Service in Scottsdale, Arizona, is a full-service agency specializing in travel throughout Indian areas nationwide, as well as in the Southwest. They can put you in touch with many specialized and personalized Indian hospitality programs that would be of interest to families. For more information, call 602/945-0771, or write to the Native American Travel Center, 4130 N. Goldwater Blvd. #114, Scottsdale, AZ 85251.

When visiting a reservation, certain rules and regulations should be observed. While they may differ somewhat, in essence the different protocols are simply examples of basic good manners.

A great source of information is the book *Indian Reservations, A State and Federal Handbook*, compiled by the Federation of American Indians, 1986, McFarland & Company, New York. This guide discusses history and culture as well as climate, transportation, and recreational facilities.

Please let us know about **your** favorite family reunion spot or adventure. Perhaps we will include it here in the next edition of this book, or in the Scrapbook Section in the back.

CHAPTER 12

Family Associations:
Advantages of Being Legal

*Why a Family Association? – Purposes of a Family Association –
Is an Association for You? – Getting Started – Surname
Associations – Sources for More Information.*

Why a Family Association?

Once you have organized a couple of successful reunions, and have discovered both interest and leadership ability in your group, you might consider forming a *family association*. To do so legally, requires that you draw up by-laws, file articles of incorporation with your state government, file for tax-exempt status with the IRS, and elect a board of directors.

In a family association, the leadership for your family projects—including reunions—shifts from an individual or small group to an elected board with appointed committees. This is similar to a small business expanding into a corporation. There are some advantages to making this move, other

than legal. First, it's easier for a family association to continue
with its projects if a leader dies or loses interest. Another is
that in the long run, more people will volunteer both time and
money to help a legal organization than a one-person show.
This is especially true of new-comers joining an organization
that's already in existance.

Purposes of a Family Association

The LDS church, which encourages its members to form
family associations, published the following list of reasons to
create an association. It could very well speak to all families.

✓ To foster love and understanding among family members.

✓ To do family research, compile records, and avoid duplica-
tion of research.

✓ To produce something to leave future generations.

✓ To preserve family records and memorablia, store keepsakes, photographs, valuable papers, and documents.

✓ To share finances for genealogical research, thereby
improving the quality of research.

✓ To make copies of the results of all research and provide
them to family members.

✓ To hold annual meetings or reunions where all can meet
and share their common bond.

Other, more specific, reasons might be:

✓ To preserve the family homestead.

✓ To create a museum housing family keepsakes and genealogical research.

✓ To create a scholarship fund for needy or deserving students.

✓ To create an endowment fund to provide donations to
churches, schools, the arts, science—whatever is dear to
the hearts of the family.

✓ To preserve a family cemetery.

Is an Association for You?

Families of any size can form an association. You should decide whether you have the need, interest, finances, and resources to run one. Some serious discussion and commitments must be made before tackling such a project.

After determining that there is reason to create an association, and that it can be administrated and financed, then decide what families will initially be included. Usually the descendants of a common ancestor or married couple are chosen. For example, it may be the first person or couple who immigrated to this country. If such a choice makes the group too large to administrate, a more recent ancestor can be selected. This ancestor may be your grandfather or a great-grandparent. If in doubt, start with a smaller group and expand.

Getting Started

Often the first plans for a family association start at a family reunion. If attendance represents most of the family branches, a decision to start an association can be brought to a vote at the reunion.

For early input, send a mailer before the reunion describing your intentions. Include a survey form for each family to write comments and mail back. From this data, you can determine if voting on an association at the reunion is appropriate.

Surname Associations

Surname associations are family associations that are open to anyone with a common last name. Some of these groups have hundreds of officers and thousands of members. Christine Rose of the Rose Family Association explains:

> A family does not have to be related to have a successful reunion. Surname organizations, for instance, have many members who are not related. It's important that people feel welcome; that those coming alone have a place to meet others. If meeting at a hotel or motel, a hospitality suite is a must, and should be open at least two days before the start of the event. For those who are not related, there must be something that will bring them together. Our association makes available 8–10 huge scrapbooks of newspaper items on Roses collected over the years.

It should be noted that related families can have their family reunions at these surname gatherings.

Sources for More Information

We have chosen to go no further into the subject of family associations in this book because a very fine book on the subject already exists:

If you are serious about starting a family association, get *Family Associations: Organization and Management* by Christine Rose. It's written by a person who has "been there," tells you everything you need to know, and includes sample by-laws. See pp. 214–15 for ordering information.

Another important book is *Starting and Running a Nonprofit Organization* by Joan Hummel. This book gives you the legal details. See the Appendix for ordering information.

CHAPTER 13

Finding People:
Solving the Mystery

*Diligence and Persistence – Find a "Sherlock" – Covering Costs –
Grapevine Leads – Using the Media – Using Our Registry –
Historic Sources – Database Searches / The Forwarded Letter –
Public Records – Using Home Computers – The Telephone as
Detective – Searching with Mailers.*

Diligence and Persistence

Depending on the family, "finding people" can be easy, hard, or seemingly take forever. Some families are so small or so tight-knit that locating people is not a problem; everybody knows where everybody is. Other families may be looking only for a few cousins who "disappeared years ago." Still others may conduct an on-going, world-wide search for anyone with a particular last name.

This chapter is limited to the basics of finding people and does not pretend to get beyond the beginner stage. For those of you needing more information—especially for genealogy searches—we refer you to the resources listed in the Appendix. Also, note two good books on finding people, p. 214.

The truth is, it takes a lot of hard work and persistence to find "missing" people. More than 99% of the information you are looking for is in someone's memory or in some file or computer somewhere in the country. It's just a question of how to get to it. *Diligence and persistence are the name of this game.*

Find a "Sherlock"

To really dig for those "hard-to-finds," it takes someone with curiosity, a knack for detective work, and persistence in following leads. Some people hate to do this and some people love it. Find someone who loves it and give them the authority and resources they need. You may find that some of these "Sherlocks" are not interested in helping with the reunion in any other way. This should be okay with you as long as they get results. Offer a "Sherlock Holmes" award during your reunion program to the person who finds the most people. This could be a joke prize such as a toy detective kit or a more serious award, such as a plaque or trophy.

One person should be in charge of finding people and their name, address, and phone number should be in all your mailings and correspondence. If possible, give this person year-round authority and funding to do research by mail and telephone. And, of course, they should be willing and able to do such research. Such a person (or persons, if you are lucky enough to have more than one in your family) is one of your greatest assets.

Professional genealogists are located throughout the U.S. and many of them will search their local public records and libraries for you. For information on finding professional genealogists, see the Appendix.

Covering Costs

The money budgeted for finding people usually pays for actual expenses such as telephone calls, mail costs, and search fees. You might pay for some gas and travel expenses, depending on the particular situation. Since the job is voluntary, labor costs (hourly wages) are almost never covered.

However, you should understand that it *does* take money to find people; and the harder and longer you look, the more it will cost per "found" person. When your group is small, every "find" is a minor celebration and the money is considered well-spent. But later on, as leads and interest wear thin, the cost per "found" person may become too high. Every year, your family should re-evaluate its policy, funding, and techniques for finding people. By taking this periodic "long, hard look," your family can optimize the interest and resources it has, and change accordingly.

Since most people must use their own phones, they may shy away from a volunteer job that costs them money. These days even dialing Directory Assistance costs money. It's necessary to budget for telephone calls as part of the reunion expense, and to let volunteers know they can be reimbursed. It's also a good idea to put a limit on the cost (or time) of each long distance call since some people may find it awkward to cut short a conversation with a long-lost relative. A set limit will give them an excuse to keep the conversation brief. You might also have a policy that if they exceed the time limit, they pay for the additional charges. Of course, these budgeting considerations require them to keep a list of the phone calls they make. If anyone in your group has access to an outgoing WATS line, you might see if it can be used in the evenings or on weekends.

"Grapevine" Leads

The "grapevine" will be your greatest source of information, especially if you learn to ask the right questions. The most important point to remember, and get across to others, is that *any small clue can help.*

In many instances, a relative or former friend may have the information necessary to find a person—they just don't realize that their knowledge is useful. In some cases, the combined information from two or three people may eventually lead to a "find." It's the searcher's job to orchestrate this process and coax people to give the information. The searcher must be willing to constantly ply people with questions that will lead to useable answers: "Do you remember what school she went to?" "Do you recall his middle name?" "What was his father's occupation?" "Did she marry someone from her hometown?" The usefulness of extracting this type of information cannot be over-emphasized. If done right, asking the right questions can lead to 80–90% of the people you are trying to find.

When talking to someone about a particular "missing" family member, ask for information on the topics in the following list. Give copies of this list to all the people helping you search and ask them to keep it by the phone.

LIST OF INFORMATION TO ASK FOR:
1. Hometown or hometown area.
2. Schools attended, years graduated.
3. Special interests or training.
4. Approximate age, if not exact birthdate.
5. Parent's occupations.
6. Nickname and middle name.
7. Religious affiliation.
8. Married name, approximate date and place of marriage.
9. Community affiliation and service clubs (Elk's, 4-H, Lion's, PTA, etc.)

ALSO, ASK THE PERSON YOU ARE TALKING TO:
1. Do you have any old photos? (Look for names, dates and other information written on the back.)
2. Do you have any old letters or diaries that might mention names or help you remember?

Note: When talking with a stranger, always mention that your purpose for finding the person is to notify them about a family reunion. And remember the first rule of finding someone: If you can't find the person directly, find someone who *can* find them.

The "hometown" lead. If you know a person's hometown, and if that community is relatively small, you have a big advantage. A letter or phone call to the mayor's office or library will secure the names of the local high schools. Get the names of the newspapers while you are at it. Write or call the school secretaries requesting a check of school records (of course, it helps to know the approximate year of graduation or age if the person didn't graduate). Any address you receive from a school will be the parents' or guardians' address at the time the person was in school, which could be very old and useless. However, the school record can also yield some very useful information, such as full name, birthdate, full names of parents, and their occupations.

Be sure to ask the school secretary for addresses and phone numbers of reunion organizers for class reunions plus-or-minus 8 years from the year your relative graduated. Class reunions are great sources of information and the organizers have done the work for you. The "plus-or-minus 8 years" allows you to find siblings or cousins with the same last name. Of course, this works best with unusual or uncommon last names.

Let's say you find the parents' first names and the father's occupation. You could place an ad in the local paper that reads like this: "Looking for James Q. Doe and family, age 48, graduate of Hometown High School, class of '61, son of John and Mary Doe, father employed as carpenter. Please write: (give address) or call collect (give phone number)." The father's occupation helps in this case because all the retired carpenters and the retired carpenters' wives are going to be racking their brains trying to remember John Doe who had a son named James. In this instance, another source worth tracking down is the local carpenters' union.

You can find the name and address of any newspaper or magazine in the U.S. through *Gale's Directory of Publications* (formerly *Ayer's* or *IMS Directory of Publications*) in your local library. These directories are indexed by location (as well as other ways), so you don't need to know the name of the newspaper in order to find the address.

Members of ethnic or close-knit religious groups within a community are very likely to be in touch with each other, at least through the "grapevine." You might want to check with a church, temple, or synagogue which the family may belong to, or contact ethnic or community organizations, especially those offering memberships and newsletters.

If someone in your family lives in the area, and has the time and inclination, she could go to an old address to ask the neighbors for information on the person being sought. Just the name of the town the person moved to could be of help. (See list of topics to cover, p. 160). Speaking with neighbors usually works if the family lived in the neighborhood for a long time. See how to do such a search using city directories on p. 164.

Using the Media

Putting a reunion announcement in the newspaper is another way to contact missing family members. However, getting an announcement printed free of charge is not likely and not easy. Most large daily newspapers will not print them, though there are exceptions to this rule. In some papers they are gathered together and printed all at once. Smaller newspapers, especially the local weeklies, are more obliging. A few regional magazines will use reunion announcements as "fillers." Most notable among these is *Yankee Magazine* which covers the New England area.

You should send a reunion announcement to a newspaper in the form of a press release as shown in Figure 29. Notice that the press release contains only the pertinent facts. Editors appreciate succinct, complete information. If, for some reason, you think a particular publication may be interested in more information for an article, either inquire first or send the information separately from your short press release.

If your press release is cut to a bare-bones minimum (as in Figure 29), it can also be used as a public service announcement (PSA) for radio stations. (It's even okay to keep the title of "press release.") However, keep in mind that most radio stations are not interested in airing family reunion announcements. If they have any interest in reunions at all, it's usually in school reunions, though there may be exceptions to this rule. The best way to get the phone numbers and addresses of radio stations is in the Yellow Pages under "Radio Stations." Otherwise look under station call letters in the very front of the "K's" or "W's" in the white pages ("C's" in Canada).

The only TV stations that will carry reunion announcements are the small local cable stations. Look under "Television Stations" in the Yellow Pages.

```
PRESS RELEASE
For release: Immediately
Contact: John Jones (717) 555-3333

Johnson Family Reunion

Descendents of Jonah and Anne Johnson of Albany.

To be held Sept. 12-13, 1993 at Sander's Park,

Yourtown, NY. Contact: John Jones, 333 Oak St.,

Pineville, PA 19123, (717) 555-3333.
```

FIGURE 29. Send a press release only to publications with a history of printing family reunion announcements. All press releases should be typed and double-line spaced.

Using Our Registry

Reunion Research, publisher of this book, maintains a *Family Reunion Registry*. Registration is free; a search costs $5; use the form on p. 216. This registry can be used by family reunion groups to:

1. look for new or missing members.

2. join our *Advisory Council* and receive occasional surveys and questionnaires on the subject of reunions. These surveys are used to compile demographic information and to update our books. Your input would be appreciated and can be anonymous.

3. learn more about the products and services of reunion suppliers (discounts, coupons, special offers, etc.).

Note: You can sign up for any or all of the above reasons. Check the appropriate box(es) on the registration form. *You will not be put on other mailing lists without your permission.*

Historic Sources Provide Clues

Diaries, old letters, old photos, scrapbooks, and old newspaper clippings can contain useful information about missing people. Always solicit these through your newsletters and mailers, and when talking with members of your family. *Be persistent!* These items are often lying in the bottom of a trunk somewhere, completely forgotten. The owner doesn't even know they are there. However, when "bothered" enough times, they may actually look for them.

If you are looking for someone who you *know* was in the military anytime between WWII and the present, get Lt Col Johnson's book listed on p. 214.

Database Searches/The Forwarded Letter

All colleges, trade schools, large corporations, unions, fraternal organizations, military publications, the Department of Veterans Affairs, military associations, etc., have databases (files) containing addresses of members, former members, alumni, employees, etc. Often these files can be searched if you provide a stamped envelope to be forwarded to the person you are looking for.

The procedure is to write a letter to the person you are looking for and place the letter in a stamped envelope with the missing person's name on the outside of the envelope. Also write on the envelope your return address and the words, "Address Correction Requested" (explained on p. 68), in the lower left corner. Send this envelope to the person or department in charge of the database, along with a note giving all identifying information about the person in question. If applicable, include the search fee. If the search is successful, the person's last known address will be written on your envelope, and the envelope mailed. (*Note:* Some organizations prefer the envelope to be sealed. Others want the envelope to be unsealed, so they can see the contents. If in doubt, leave it unsealed, or ask for their procedures first.) Furnish as much identifying information as possible.

This "forwarded letter" approach is one of the best investments available. The cost is two stamps, two envelopes, and some paper. Be sure to include all pertinent information in a cover letter to the organization that has the database. It really helps to throw in some phrases like: "last resort," "I've been looking for this person for 5 years," "you're my only hope," "I know you are extremely busy, but....," etc.

The "forwarded letter" procedure protects the privacy of the individual. You cannot learn their address unless they decide to respond to your letter. *A word to the wise:* Don't be discouraged when a letter is not answered. Some people just aren't enthusiastic about reunions or may have reasons not to respond.

Public Records

Registrar of voters. This is by far the easiest and most productive public record to access, and it's free. These records are kept at county government offices. Remember that most people live within 50 miles of where they grew up. If there is another county nearby, check those records, too.

Department of Motor Vehicles. Each state has its own name for this department; you are looking for the drivers license records. In most states, this information, or at least the address and phone number, is available to the public. However, you will probably need the birthdate as well as the full name before they will conduct a search. There is almost always a charge ranging from 75¢ to $6 per search, regardless of its success. The following states need either the person's written permission, or the driver's license number, which means that requesting information from them is useless: Alabama, Arkansas, California, Georgia, Hawaii, Idaho, Illinois, Iowa, Kansas, Missouri, and Pennsylvania. These states do not allow a driver's license check of any kind: Massachusetts and Washington (state).

County tax office or assessor's office. This is where title insurance firms get their information, but of course they can access all the counties of the state. These files are usually not computerized which means that you will have to physically look through them. Often they are on microfiche. Sometimes there is an hourly charge to look.

County recorder's office. Grantee/grantor records are held at the county level, and include deeds, power of attorney papers, real estate transactions, liens, and anything officially recorded on paper between two or more people. When confronted with these files, don't be overwhelmed by the legal jargon, just make a note of the information that you can use: addresses, full names, children's names, occupation, legal advisers, business partners, etc.

Marriage records. Most younger people apply for a marriage license in the county where they grew up, and many women are married in their home community. These records are kept at the county level and are especially good for finding women's married names. In some states and for various reasons, these records may be "sealed."

Vital statistics records. Birth and death statistics are first recorded at the county level, but a copy is usually sent to the state government. For local information, go to the county court house. If you are dealing with a distant county or another state, first try the Department of Health, the Department of Human Resources, or the Office of Vital Statistics at the state capital. Each state calls it something different. If they don't have the information you seek, they can tell you how to get it and how much it will cost. The fees range from $1 to $6 per search.

Business license records. Business licenses are recorded at the city and county level. Since about half the population eventually starts a business of its own, this can be a rewarding source. A fictitious business name must be registered by anyone doing business under any name other than their given legal name.

Using Home Computers

As a result of developing technology in personal computers and telecommunications, Electronic Bulletin Board Services (BBS's) have come into existence in the last few years. They are owned and operated by particular "interest groups," and are usually run from people's homes on personal computers (PC's)—at no financial gain. With these services, anyone owning a personal computer, a telephone, and a modem can leave ("post") messages or receive messages, as you would on a bulletin board. From the comfort of your own computer desk, you can leave a reunion announcement, search for a reunion announcement, announce that you are looking for a specific person or persons, gather helpful information, or ask any question. Then you can check in from time to time to see if anyone has left a message for you in response. The only cost is for long distance phone calls. For families, the most likely sources are the "genealogy BBS's." See the Appendix for information on how to find these phone numbers.

Commercial Electronic Networks. These are subscription services that are like huge BBS's, but commercially operated. You usually pay a one-time sign up fee plus so much per hour for log-on time. Some also have a monthly charge. Thousands of people belong to these services, and the equipment can handle hundreds of calls at a time. Once inside these databases, you will find many areas of interest. "Genealogy Forums" are maintained by CompuServe and GEnie, and perhaps others. See the Appendix for more information. An interesting feature is the ability to have a "live discussion" (typed on the computer screen) on a particular subject with many different people at once. Messages (questions, answers, and statements) appear on the screen in the order sent by the people involved in the discussion. The topics and times of these discussions are announced weeks ahead of time and are led by experts on the subject being discussed.

The Telephone as Detective

When looking through phone books, and when calling Directory Assistance, remember that the main objective is to get the address. The phone number is important, too, but your first attempt at contact should be through the mail. It will be cheaper to mail the information, and besides, you have to send the reunion mailers anyway. Use the telephone if the person doesn't respond to the mailing (it may be that the address is incorrect and the envelope was not returned), or if the person is "found" just before the reunion and has no time to receive your notice.

When using phone books, of course you should check under the full name of the person. But also check for possible relatives, especially if it's an unusual or uncommon name. This may be hopeless for a Smith or a Johnson, but let's say you are looking for a Kradowsky. You notice a Kradowsky in the phone book, but the first name is wrong. You phone that particular Kradowsky and find that the person you are looking for is his first cousin who moved to Pittsburgh, PA, ten years ago and they have been out of touch. Next, dial "00" (long distance operator) and ask for the area code for Pittsburgh, PA. Then dial the area code plus 555-1212 for information in Pittsburgh. (Remember, you will be charged a small fee for directory assistance calls.)

All public and college libraries have a large assortment of current phone books from the major metropolitan areas around the country. To save yourself a lot of time, phone first to find out if they have the ones you need. Libraries or sections within libraries that are specifically designed for genealogical research (tracing family history) have truly amazing collections of both out-of-date and current phone books and city directories. For example, the Sutro Library in San Francisco, which is by no means the largest, has on hand 15,000 city directories and 10,000 telephone books. For genealogical libraries in your area, look under "Libraries" in the Yellow Pages. Your state library system, LDS Family History Centers, and the National Archives System should be the best sources. See the Appendix for more information.

City directories (sometimes called criss-cross directories) are published by private companies and contain two separate listings: alphabetical by name and numerical by street address. The alphabetical listing often includes the person's occupation, but you will have to turn to the address listing to find the phone number. Occasionally, unlisted phone numbers are found here.

With the help of a street map that shows the street numbers, you can find the phone numbers of neighbors. Then by comparing the old city directories with the new, you can figure out who is still living in the neighborhood. When you call, remember to mention that it is for a family reunion. Also, leave your name and phone number with them in case they remember something later. If you are really persistent, call back in a week or two to see if they have remembered something after having had a chance to think about it.

Let's say you find a name you are looking for in a phone book. Even the middle name or initial is the same, and you are reasonably sure the person is (or was) somewhere in the area. You phone the number and are informed the number is disconnected or no longer in service. Don't give up! Call Directory Assistance to see if another number is listed. The number published may not be right. The person may have recently moved and the phone company erred in referring the number. If that doesn't work, send a postcard to the address in the phone book (if one is listed). Remember, if the person moved, the Post Office is likely to forward mail longer than the phone company is likely to refer the phone number. Next, follow the instructions on p. 171–72 for sending a letter to the current resident asking her help. Persistence is the name of this game.

The cheapest times to call long distance are usually from 11 p.m. to 8 a.m., all day Saturday and Sunday until 5 p.m. (local time). But it depends on the rules of your long distance carrier.

"Reach Out America" is a money saving plan by AT&T, and is primarily designed for additional savings during the already low-rate times. These low-rate times (all day Saturday and Sunday until 5 p.m.) are a good time to reach families anyway. There are three levels to this program, with the highest level saving you money any time you call. This is called the "24-hour plan" and also includes international calls. For more information, call 800/222-0300. Of course, your long distance carrier must be AT&T. Other carriers may have money saving plans, too. Call to find out.

Some interesting facts about unlisted phone numbers:

✓ Over 40% of all residential phone numbers are unlisted, and the more affluent a person, the more likely the number is unlisted.

✓ Sometimes an unlisted number will appear in a city directory.

✓ Directory Assistance in some areas (it depends on the rules of the local phone company) will tell you if the name you are looking for has an unpublished (unlisted) number. You won't get the number, but at least you know that the person (or a person with that name) is in the area. Unfortunately this convenience is slowly being phased out all over the country.

Dealing with Directory Assistance. Some information operators are not very personable, and many of them are talking to each other between calls (and, therefore, not giving you their full attention). In addition, they must average a certain number of calls per hour, so they are not too anxious to "linger" while you collect your thoughts when the name you ask for doesn't immediately turn up.

Our experience in the last twelve years has been that Directory Assistance is wrong or misleading about 10% of the time. Sometimes operators give you the wrong number (if you report this back to an operator, you will get credit for the call). Other times the name is there; they just can't find it. Or more precisely, they don't check various spellings or initials; they look only under the exact name and spelling you ask for and if it's not there, you lose. There is no way for you to know if they are checking other options or not. So you have to be explicit. If you ask, for example, for the number of a David Charles MacKenzie, and are informed that it's not there, then ask for "initials D.C.," "initial D.," "D. Charles," and MacKenzie spelled with "Mc" instead of "Mac." If you are very interested in finding a person, you should try Directory Assistance more than once. You are likely to get another operator next time you call.

You are usually allowed three directory checks (sometimes two, depending on the area) per phone call to Directory Assistance, but you must tell the operator first that you are looking for more than one number. Then you will get the first number(s) by live human voice and the last by an electronic voice called an audio response unit.

Many people don't realize that in most areas it is possible (and legitimate) to get an address from the Directory Assistance operator. Obviously, this could ultimately save you a phone call. You must ask for the address right from the start. You will get the address (or be informed that there is no address listed) from a live operator before being turned over to the electronic voice for the phone number.

Using the telephone is a personal approach. This can be a great advantage. A real live voice on the other end of the line is a lot different from a notice in the mail, and can easily elicit the "nostalgic interest" necessary for the person to say "Yes, I want to be there!" We suggest phoning all the "nonresponses" 6 to 8 weeks before the reunion. A good time is right after the last mailer is sent. If possible, have someone call who "best knows" the family or person being called.

Using the phone in this way can definitely be cost-effective. If you convince only five extra people to attend, at $20 each that's $100. And at the very least, you get to verify some addresses in your "unverified" address file.

Searching with Mailers

Be sure to include a list of missing persons in every mailer and newsletter you send out. In addition, make a plea for help in locating people. It's easy for people to forget about notifying you or put it off until later, assuming that someone else will do it. Mention in the mailer that the reader may very well be the only one with information on a particular individual, and not to assume someone else will send in the information.

Make it easy for people to contact you. Include a phone number (two, if possible) in all your mailers. Some people are very impulsive and "phone oriented." They will make a call, but won't take the time to write. Give the phone numbers of people who 1) are willing and able to field phone calls, 2) are reasonably gregarious and enthusiastic, 3) are near the phone much of the time, especially in the evening, and 4) have a phone answering machine.

Old addresses are often wrong. But if you can't get an address in any other way, send an announcement to an old address. Remember, if it's not sent back by return mail, you can't assume the addressee received it. The person now living at that address (if it slipped past the Post Office's mail forwarding system—which is quite possible) may have thrown it away. Also, "mail forwarding" is good for only one year at the most, and in metropolitan areas, 6 months. You might consider writing a letter to the "occupant" or "resident" of the address to see if they know the whereabouts of the person you are looking for. The exact address may not be known, but they may know the city to which your relatives moved. Ask for clues (give a list), hand-address the envelope and write "Important!!" and "Personal" on the outside (since many people throw away letters addressed to "occupant"), and include a self-addressed, stamped postcard or ask them to call you collect. And always mention that it's for a reunion.

More information on mailing and postage is available in Chapter 6.

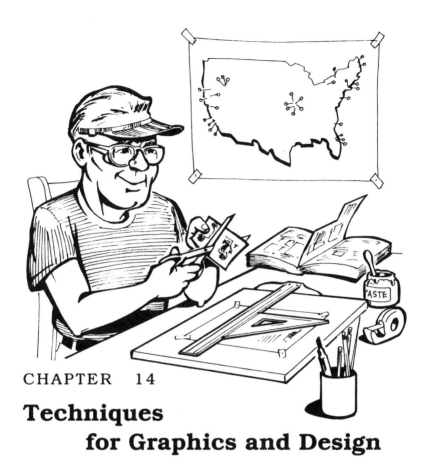

CHAPTER 14

Techniques
for Graphics and Design

Letterheads – Creating the Originals – Columnized Format –
Tools of the Trade – Graphics Tips – Include Entertainment –
Desktop Publishing.

Anything that is put into printed form—mailers, newsletters, surveys, questionnaires—can benefit from learning a few graphics and design techniques. Such techniques are not that hard to learn, and the tools needed are inexpensive (until you get into computers). This chapter has many paste-up, layout, and design tips. More information is available from the resources, catalogs, and books mentioned in the Appendix, especially the Dot Graphics Supply catalog. Also, your local library is a good place for further information—there is no lack of printed material on the subject.

Letterheads

A nice touch for mailers and newsletters is to create a good looking letterhead or logo. An artist in the family could design it, or a typesetter or commercial artist could develop one. Since you can use the original copy of a letterhead over and over again, this would be a one-time expense. For added interest, the letterhead can be printed in a color different than the text by using the technique described on p. 183.

BULLETIN
OF THE
FRISBIE — FRISBEE FAMILY
ASSOCIATION OF AMERICA

NEWS

HARDEN NEWSLETTER

𝕳arðs 𝕱amilp
NEWSLETTER

Number 13

JANUARY 1991

THE LAND - 1661   THE HOMESTEAD BUILT - 1803
THE ASSOCIATION INCORPORATED - 1962
TAX DEDUCTIBLE STATUS - 1965

The EDDY   # HOMESTEADER

NEWSLETTER FROM THE EDDY HOMESTEAD ASSOCIATION, INC.

FIGURE 30. Examples of family newsletter letterheads. The letterhead of the Eymann Family Newsletter was printed in red ink using the technique described on p. 183. The text of the newsletter was in black ink.

Creating the Originals

The final copy of your mailer or newsletter, the one you take to the printer, is referred to as the "original." To create the original, it's best to use a professional quality typewriter, preferably with a carbon ribbon. If your typewriter uses only fabric ribbons, put in a fresh ribbon and clean out the o's and e's. You want a crisp, dark print that will reproduce well. If you have a choice of type styles, "Letter Gothic" from IBM is ideal. Stay away from "Script" type faces. They are popular, but they don't reproduce well and they become tedious to read.

When creating your originals, type on only one side of a sheet of paper. It will be "backed" or "double sided" (printed on both sides of one sheet) at the print or copy shop. If you are doing any "cutting and pasting" (see p. 177 for definition), use paste-up boards for a lay-out guide. Available at graphic art supply stores, they are very inexpensive (about 50¢ each), and have guidelines printed in nonreproducible ("nonrepro") blue ink. Use a glue stick or spray adhesive to stick the original work to the paste-up boards (cellophane tape can give inferior results).

Drawings, cartoons, and border designs can add interest to your paper. Dover Books has clip art books on many topics. They are full of pictures and designs you can cut out and paste to create borders or add graphics between articles. Graphic supply houses usually sell Dover Books or you can ask your local bookstore to order them for you. Children's line drawings, if distinct, work well. However, don't add so many graphics that you crowd your pages.

After the originals are finished, quick printing or photocopying is the next step. Unless you are mailing a very small quantity, quick printing may be less expensive and probably better looking, especially if you are including photographs. However, the latest models of Xerox and Canon photocopiers can give excellent results. Get several bids from printers and photocopy shops and *be sure to compare quality*. (See the Yellow Pages under "Printers," or "Copying and Duplicating Services.") "Home copiers" or those found in supermarkets and libraries often make poor quality copies.

For a price, the process of folding, three-hole punching, or stapling can be done by the print shop. If your family will be saving newsletters in a binder, three-hole punching is a nice feature to provide.

Columnized Format

There are many basic formats that a newsletter can follow. The Appendix lists books that provide good examples. Find a format that appeals to your aesthetic sense, but don't feel that it must be adhered to issue after issue. There's nothing wrong with changing the design of your newsletter as you learn more about typography and graphics.

In its simplest form, a piece of typing paper can be filled margin-to-margin. The only problem with this is that it makes for tedious reading. The longer the line of type, the harder it is for the eye to track back to the beginning of the next line. For this reason, columns have been invented. Figure 7B on p. 61 shows a simple two-column format. The instructions below explain how to create such a format:

```
This is what regular typing looks like. It's
large, takes up a lot of space, and looks like
a business letter. To dress up your mailers and
newsletters, you can try the following tricks:
```

```
Columnize your format. If the final result
will be printed on 8 1/2 x 11 paper, then
two columns side by side are probably
best. If you have a 1/2" margin on both
sides plus a 1/2" between columns, then
each column will be 3 1/2" wide. Elite
type looks better or you can have it
reduced (below).
```

```
If you have your original type reduced down to 80%
it will look even better. But to get the final re-
sult 3 1/2" wide, that means your original should be
4 3/8" wide. So type it up, take it to a copy shop,
and have it reduced to 80%. It'll cost about 25
cents per sheet. Paste it up and add some other in-
teresting things such as separators, borders and
clip art, all of which you can find at an art store
that has graphic supplies.
```

You can also use asterisks for separators, like this:

```
        *       *       *       *       *

or just draw a short line like this:

        _____

or throw in a fancy store-bought one like this:

        _____◄●►_____
```

Another neat trick is to capitalize the first letter of each article by using some "rub on" type or transfer lettering that you can buy at an art store. Make sure you get the right size letters. As a guide, type a couple of lines on your typewriter and take them to the store. A letter that's a little too big looks better than one that's too small. You can also apply the letter after the copy has been reduced.

YOU CAN BEGIN EACH ARTICLE with about a half line of capitalized type. The capitalized part should include a complete phrase or idea, and not be chopped off anywhere.

Tools of the Trade

Cutting and pasting your original together to get it ready for the printer or photocopier is called "paste-up." Graphic artists use all sorts of expensive equipment to do this, most of which you don't need. However, it helps to have:

✓ paste-up boards or planning paper. These are printed with "nonrepro blue" guide lines and are used to create (paste-up) the original. They come in different weights, sizes, and grids, and are useful for aligning the work properly (Figure 31). A good selection is available from Dot Paste-Up Supply and their catalog tells you everything you need to know (see the Appendix). However, their minimum order is 100 sheets. Smaller quantities are available from graphic art stores.

✓ a triangle with a right angle, preferably of clear plastic. This is to get the copy lined up level, and to provide a straight edge for the razor blade. A small T-square will also work.

✓ razor blades (single edge) or X-acto knife.

✓ scissors.

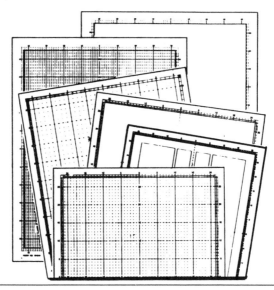

FIGURE 31. Layout boards are one of the secrets to creating good look-ing mailers and newsletters. There are many different grids and sizes, but all are printed in "nonrepro" blue (depicted here in black).

✓ a blue pencil. Used to make marks or notes on the original that won't show up on the final result. Ask for a nonrepro blue pencil (not pen) at a graphic arts store.

✓ white-out liquid. Comes in a small bottle with applicator. Commonly used to cover typing errors and will get rid of "shadow lines" which are the result of paper edges showing up when the original is photocopied.

✓ something to cut on when you use the razor blade. Don't use the kitchen table or anything you don't want to cut up. Use masonite (hardboard), good quality plywood without knots or cracks, glass, marble, etc. Glass works best.

✓ masking tape. Used to hold down the original while you are working on it.

✓ glue, wax, or spray adhesive. Used to hold the various pieces down on the original. If you use glue or cellophane tape, it's difficult to pick up a piece and re-set it (in case you make a mistake or change your mind). Done professionally, it is pasted down with wax because wax allows you to pick up a piece and re-set it as many times as you like. However, the cheapest little hand-held waxer is $45 (they are electric in order to melt the wax)—a good investment if you can afford it. However, for mailers or small newsletters, the best bet is to paste-up with either a wax stick (like a lipstick) for around $3, or nonpermanent spray adhesive for about $10 a can.

Or you might consider purchasing the "Office Paste-Up Kit" offered by Dot Paste-Up Supply for around $65. It includes all of the above plus some. See the Appendix.

Graphics Tips

✓ You can get more printing onto the paper by reducing the original down to 75–80%. This can be done photographically for $4–5 per photo (called a PMT or velox) or on some photocopying machines for about 25¢ per copy. The quality won't be as good if photocopied, but should be good enough. Make your original the proper size so that the reduced copy fits into the required space. For example, an original of 10" x 10" when reduced to 80% of its original size will be 8" x 8" (100% means the same size as the original).

✓ 11 x 17 folded in half comes out to $8\frac{1}{2}$ x 11. This makes a nice newsletter size that can be opened like a magazine. The print shop can fold it for you at extra cost.

✓ "Rub-on" type and transfer lettering can be bought at graphics supply stores. Type can be used to create letterheads, headlines, or any "line of type" that is to appear in large or stylized letters. They come in hundreds of styles and many sizes. Graphic art stores have catalogs of type styles that you can read at home. You may find it too confusing to pick a type style at the store. The store may also have giveaway "how-to" pamphlets.

✓ Kroy lettering machines are available for customer use at some copy shops. These machines put out a tape of "headlines" in different styles and size of type. The operator turns a wheel that points to each letter in succession, and slowly but surely the heading is created. Prices are very inexpensive, starting at about 30¢ per inch.

✓ "Clip art" is any line image or drawing (not a photograph or halftone) that can be used to enhance a printed work. The

FIGURE 32. *Clip art and transfer lettering can help make your mailers and newsletters more interesting. Examples like these and thousands more are available from graphic art stores and mail order suppliers.*

most common examples are a hand with pointing finger and a hand with scissors. See Figure 32 for examples. These usually come in books or sheets, available at graphic art stores. You clip them out (hence the name) and paste them onto your "original." However, the cheapest source is magazines, newspapers, and telephone yellow pages. If you find something you like, but it's the wrong size, it can be made larger or smaller by using photocopiers that can enlarge or reduce. Other clip art examples are decorative borders, banners, frames, arrows, symbols, etc. A catalog will give you more ideas. Send for catalogs from Dot Paste-Up Supply, The Printer Shopper, or the manufacturer (see the Appendix).

✓ Any image (clip art, photos, borders, headings) can be enlarged or reduced in most photocopy machines. The trick is to find the right machine; some machines only reduce. Others have only two or three settings (for example, 64%, 78%, and 120%). Some have incremental settings of 1 or 1/2 percent. All of them have range limits (for example: 64–142%). The Kodak IM40 has a wide range from 36–400%. Since you want to avoid making copies of copies as much as possible (especially with photos), call around to find a machine that will give you what you want in one "shot." The better copy shops have several machines available, each machine specializing in different functions.

✓ Most photocopy machines are designed to not "see" the color blue. This can be a problem when trying to photocopy letters written in (or signed in) blue ink (see Figure 33). The best cure is prevention. When soliciting letters that will be reproduced, give instructions to use black or red ink (red shows up as black). If it's just a signature in blue ink, you can carefully trace over it with black ink. Otherwise, try to find a photocopy machine that can "see" blue. Also, setting the contrast control for "darker" can help.

✓ If you can't get good results when photocopying photos, try using a "copy screen." This is a transparent plastic film with tiny white dots that break up the solid blackness in the photo. Lay it down on the glass in the photocopy machine and place the photo face down over it. The better copy shops will have these screens available, but check first. Otherwise, they can be purchased at graphic art stores. Some of the very latest copy machines now have a "photo" setting. This makes use of an internal type of copy screen.

✓ If you are including photos in a mailer or newsletter, the quality will be better if you use the quick-print method instead of photocopying.

✓ Color photos can be reproduced as black-and-white, but the results are always a little muddy. Any time photos are taken that will be reproduced in black-and-white (for newspapers, candid photos in the newsletter, etc.) use black-and-white film.

✓ When getting multiple copies made at a copy shop, *always* check the first copy for shadow lines, specks, misalignment, etc., before giving the go-ahead on the others. (See Figure 33.) Take a bottle of white-out correction fluid with you. Some copy shops don't keep white-out around because people don't let it dry and it gums up the machine or speckles the glass. If shadow lines or specks appear on the first copy, use white-out on the original and try another single copy (also check the glass on the photocopy machine for specks). Be absolutely certain that the first copy is what you want before going ahead on the others. If you can't get what you want, try another copy shop. There is an amazing difference in quality among different brands and models of copy machines. How often a copy machine is serviced can affect the quality of its copies.

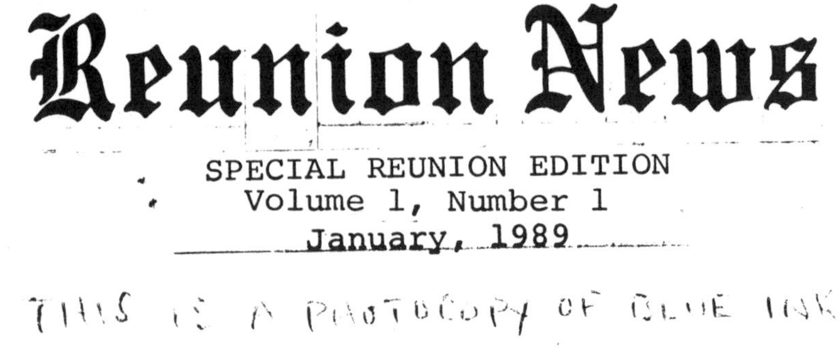

Reunion News

SPECIAL REUNION EDITION
Volume 1, Number 1
January, 1989

THIS IS A PHOTOCOPY OF BLUE INK

FIGURE 33. *Problems and mistakes such as these can easily be avoided. Use "white-out" on specks and shadow lines. Use a layout board and a triangle to properly align the "paste-up." Avoid blue ink. When doing multiple copies, always check the first copy very carefully before giving the "go ahead" on the others.*

✓ The 1025 and 1035 model Xerox copiers, Canon 6650 II, and others have interchangeable color cartridges (green, blue, red, brown and black). This allows you, for example, to have a color heading with black text (by putting the paper through the machine twice). The originals are all in black—it's the changeable cartridges that produce the different colors. If interested, call around to find a shop that has a machine with changeable colored ink cartridges. (Note: This is not the same as a "color copier," which reproduces color photos.)

Include Some Entertainment

It's fun for the reader as well as the editor to include trivia, family sayings, proverbs, quotes, jokes, cartoons, family historic dates, bits of wisdom, recipes, quizzes, puzzles, brain teasers, and items of nostalgic or historic interest (especially if they compare the past with the present). There are many books that can provide you with such information or you can ask family members to contribute. Some books are listed in the Appendix; many more can be found in your local library.

There are mail-order companies that offer "historical printouts of any date." The time span is usually from 1900 to present; the main purpose is to show people what was happening in the world on the day they were born. The price is certainly right, around $5 per printout on an $8\frac{1}{2}$ x 11 sheet. The printout of a significant date will give you enough information for three or four newsletters. Figure 34 shows an example. See the Appendix, Window In Time, for a source.

Examples of trivia:

In 19xx:
- The price of gas was ___ per gallon.
- We mailed a letter for ___.
- Bread cost ___ per loaf.
- The ballpoint pen was not yet invented.
- Credit cards did not exist.
- The Zip Code was ___ years in the future.
- *Life* magazine was ___ per copy.

You might use such a page when a couple is celebrating their 50th wedding anniversary to show what it was like when they were married. Using almanacs and encyclopedias to gather information for "What Year Was It?" is too slow (with the exception of encyclopedia annual volumes). The best chronology resources are *The Timetables of History* and *The People's Chronology*, both described in the Appendix. The best sources for creating a quiz are trivia books and games.

WINDOW IN TIME

DECEMBER 26, 1943

THIS IS HOW THE CALENDAR WOULD LOOK ON DECEMBER 26, 1943

PRESIDENT OF THE U.S. WAS FRANKLIN D. ROOSEVELT
VICE-PRESIDENT WAS HENRY A. WALLACE

DECEMBER

S	M	T	W	T	F	S
			1	2	3	4
5	6	7	8	9	10	11
12	13	14	15	16	17	18
19	20	21	22	23	24	25
26	27	28	29	30	31	

SOME PRICES IN 1943, COMPARED WITH 1986 ARE:

	1943	1986
A POUND LOAF OF BREAD	$0.09	$0.70
A HALF GALLON OF MILK	$0.31	$1.18
A POUND OF BUTTER	$0.53	$2.65
A POUND OF ROUND STEAK	$0.44	$2.69
ONE GALLON OF GASOLINE	$0.17	$1.07
A NEW FORD AUTOMOBILE	N.A.	$8,725.
AVERAGE ANNUAL INCOME	$1,951.	$21,310.

IN 1943 - THE WORLD SERIES WAS WON BY THE NEW YORK YANKEES (AL)
BEATING THE ST. LOUIS CARDINALS (NL)

MOST
POPULAR:
SONG - OH, WHAT A BEAUTIFUL MORNIN - ALFRED DRAKE
MOVIE - CASABLANCA
ACTOR - PAUL LUKAS - "WATCH ON THE RHINE"
ACTRESS - JENNIFER JONES - "THE SONG OF BERNADETTE"

SOME STORIES THAT APPEARED IN NEWSPAPERS ON OR NEAR DECEMBER 26, 1943 ARE:

12/24   GENERAL DWIGHT D. EISENHOWER WAS NAMED SUPREME COMMANDER OF THE EUROPEAN INVASION FORCES.

12/27   THE HEISMAN MEMORIAL TROPHY, FOR THE OUTSTANDING COLLEGIATE FOOTBALL PLAYER OF THE YEAR, WAS AWARDED TO ANGELO BERTELLI THE QUARTERBACK FOR NOTRE DAME. NOTRE DAME WAS THIS YEAR'S NATIONAL COLLEGE FOOTBALL CHAMPIONS.

1/7   FRANK SINATRA, THE IDOL OF THE "BOBBY-SOXERS," BEGINS AN ENGAGEMENT IN MANHATTAN'S PARAMOUNT THEATER BEFORE A SCREAMING AUDIENCE OF 30,000.

1/16   PAPER SHORTAGES CAUSED PUBLISHERS TO COME OUT WITH PAPERBACK BOOKS. THE POPULARITY WAS SO GREAT THAT THE PRACTICE NEVER ENDED.

FIGURE 34. Historical printouts are available by mail (see the Appendix). They can provide you with good information to use in your mailers, newsletters, or reunion program.

┌─────────── WHIZ QUIZ ───────────┐
What word contains the vowels in order?
              — a — e — i o u —

              (facetious)
└─────────────────────────────────┘

┌─────────── WHIZ QUIZ ───────────┐
John was standing directly behind Mary.
Mary was standing directly behind John.
          Same Mary - Same John.
          But how can that be?

(John and Mary were standing back to back)
└─────────────────────────────────┘

┌────────── WHAT YEAR WAS IT? ──────────┐
Pennsylvania Turnpike completed from
Carlisle to Irwin.   A new Chevy coupe
sells for $659.   Color TV pioneered by
CBS.   Reds win first Series, first nylon
stockings go on sale. "You are my sunshine"
popular.   Kate Hepburn stars in "Philadelphia story", Ralph Edwards introduces
"Truth or Consequences".

(1940)
└───────────────────────────────────────┘

┌────────── WHAT YEAR WAS IT? ──────────┐
Margaret Thatcher new leader of England.
Suez Canal reopens. Astronauts and Cosmo-
nauts share meals 140 miles in space. Phila-
delphia Flyers win Stanley cup. Art Carney
Oscars for Best Actor. Salmon spawn in
Connecticut River, 1st time in 100 years.

(1975)
└───────────────────────────────────────┘

FIGURE 35. Here are two ways to make your mailers or newsletters more interesting. The answers, of course, should appear on a different page than the questions.

Examples of quotes about families and ancestry:

Speaking of his ancestry Lincoln once humorously remarked, "I don't know who my grandfather was, but I am much more concerned to know what his grandson will be."

To a man who had proudly said, "My ancestors came over on the Mayflower," Will Rogers retorted, "My ancestors were waiting on the beach."

Mark Twain, whenever confronted by people who were haughty about their ancestry, was fond of saying, "My grandfather was cut down in the prime of his life. My grandmother used to say that if he had been cut down fifteen minutes earlier, he could have been revived."

Desktop Publishing

If someone in your group has a computer/software combination for desktop publishing or if someone has the knowledge of how to use one (through job experience, for example), then you can create some truly impressive mailers or newsletters for not much money.

Amazing things can be done on personal computers these days. To find out exactly what, ask for a demonstration of desktop publishing at one of your local computer stores. The most "user friendly" computer is probably the Macintosh. One of the least expensive and also "user friendly" is the Atari ST (which was used to create this book).

Newsletters and mailers can be created with dot matrix printers, but laser printers produce much higher quality (Figure 36). The good news is that you don't have to own a laser printer to use one (since they are rather expensive). If your software can "print to disk," you can take your disk (or mail it) to a typesetter or printing service bureau that will output laser printer copy for you for around $2–5 per page. *These pages become your originals from which photocopies or quick-print copies are made.*

Some computer stores also rent computers by the hour (you work at the store), but you have to know how to use the software or else you will be wasting your time and money. Some of the fancier copy or print shops around universities offer such services.

Family Reunion News

Family Reunion News

Family Reunion News

Family Reunion News

FIGURE 36. The top example was created on a 9-pin printer, the bottom on a laser printer at 300 dots per inch. The same software was used for each. The laser output can be obtained by taking the disk (or mailing it) to a printing service bureau. You don't need to purchase a laser printer.

──────── Positive Family Traits────────

Some families seem to be particularly strong, emotionally healthy, and enduring, with a minimum of internal bickering and dissention. Jane Howard, in her book *Families*, looked for the characteristic traits of such families and found the following qualities (with slight modifications by us):

● A distinguished member, a founder, someone to admire and emulate (not necessarily still living).

● A family historian or genealogist. Someone who keeps track of the clan, facilitates communication among members, maintains scrapbooks and other forms of family history.

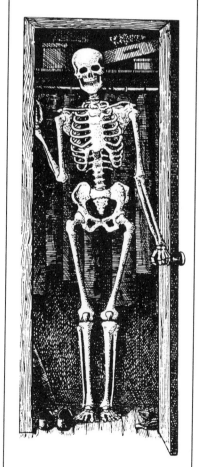

● A basic sense of humor that permeates the entire family.

● Parents and children devoted to outside pursuits as well as each other.

● Hospitable homes with friends and relatives warmly received.

● Willingness to lend aid and support in times of need.

● At least one cherished eccentric and a general tolerance for the failings of others.

● Prized rituals, both traditional (such as holiday customs) and unique celebrations (invented by the family).

● Affectionate touching, hugs, and comforting.

● A "sense of place"—if not a home then a collection of belongings that symbolize home.

● Children are included in the talk and laughter.

● Elders are honored.

(*Thanks to the Crinklaw Family for the information on this page.)

There's a skeleton in every closet!

Reunion Scrapbook

This Scrapbook Section is the direct result of us getting tired of explaining everything in text book fashion. What this book needs (we said) is some direct explanation from the people themselves. The result is the following pages.

In future editions of this book, this section will become "bigger and better." We would love to add your input to these pages. Document part of your next reunion for us. Take photos. Write an explanation of how your reunion is interesting or different. You will earn a free book for your efforts plus our enduring gratitude, not to mention the gratitude of many reunion planners who will benefit from your example.

The same goes for videos. Join our *Video Project*. Send us a copy of your reunion video showing examples of reunion activities. Even five seconds worth of an interesting activity may be of interest to us. If we add your footage to our "Reunion Activities" tape, we will send you a free copy.

FAMILY REUNION SCRAPBOOK

A Gathering of Ideas

General Description: About 200 people came to our reunion (Friday night until late Sunday), which turned out to be quite a success. We started planning and sent flyers out 14 months before the reunion. We gave some family history, asked for other addresses and contacts, mentioned some ideas, asked for suggestions, and gave the names of the primary organizers. Later we sent maps of the area along with information on campsites, motels, restaurants, recreational facilities, and what to bring.

Dähler Family Reunion 1988

Notices were sent to local papers announcing the reunion 5 to 6 weeks in advance, and another 10 days ahead. Also a notice was put in the *Genealogical Helper* a year before and also a month or two in advance of the reunion. This resulted in a family from Maryland coming, even though they didn't know for sure if they were related. (We found out later that they were.)

After the reunion we sent a wrap-up letter with thank-yous and a list of addresses. Suggestions were made to have another reunion in two years and maybe a reunion in Switzerland in five years.

S.S. Holsatia. Used courtesy of the Peabody Museum, Salem, MA

Our most popular activity was a "show & tell" session with each branch of the family telling its story to help the younger members know more about their ancestors. This included a slide presentation showing the ship our immigrant family arrived on, some photos of the family, and some letters from the family who stayed in Switzerland. There was also a map showing the family's place of origin. People came from 16 states and Switzerland.

Activities and Programs: Our immigrant couple had eight children. We asked for one person to head each branch with everyone wearing a colored ribbon to show their branch of the family. Buttons were made with the ancestors' photo on them.

We awarded small prizes to the youngest, oldest, who came the farthest, had the most grandchildren, youngest baby – anything we could think of so lots of people could get something.

Baseball and volleyball games were organized for the younger children while the adults visited with each other. We had some of the teenagers supervise.

We printed up directions to the old homestead for people who wanted to drive out and look at the area, and also directions to the cemetery with a list of family members buried there.

One member offered to print t-shirts and baseball caps with the Dahler name on them. This was a nice plus! Another person brought a camcorder and offered tapes to us after the reunion, which was also great!

Site: We rented a building in a city park very reasonably, to have a place to show slides, give awards, etc., in case of inclement weather. They often have many different types of buildings, but think well ahead. Be sure to ask about other events taking place nearby.

Potential Problems: Try to make arrangements for both smokers and nonsmokers. The 5-10 smokers felt discriminated against by having to go outside. Maybe have a separate smoking room.

Don't cram too many activities into the reunion. People want more time for socializing. Suggest planning activities for the morning, leaving the afternoon for social time.

We had a catered meal arranged for Saturday evening based on the number of people who said they were going to attend, plus a few extras "just in case." About 15 people never showed up, and those meals had to be paid for, plus what to do with all the extra food? Be sure to collect the meal money ahead of time.

MAPLE HILL FARM 1861
Mt. Angel, Oregon

The STEVENS Family Centennial Reunion 1891-1990

On June 14, 1891, five brothers and sisters — the children of Hanson and Lavina Stevens, pioneers who came to Oregon by covered wagon some 40 years earlier — met with their families at the home of the eldest brother for a family reunion. They enjoyed themselves so thoroughly that it was agreed to meet annually. A journal was purchased and the day's transactions were recorded. A tradition was then begun that has faithfully endured for over 100 years.

The Centennial Reunion Committee first met in 1987 (four years early). The structure of a history book was set with chapters, contents, authors, and timelines for completion. Decisions were made regarding the reunion, its site, publicity, announcements, activities and so forth.

Other meetings continued — perhaps one or two a year. The reunion was to take place over four days in the latter part of July (traditionally, the reunion occurred only on the third Sunday of July). The last surviving farm in the family, over 125 years old, was chosen as the venue; a family "logo" was designed for t-shirts and coffee mugs; "up-scale" announcements were printed; a Saturday barbecue followed by a lawn dance with a live band was organized.

There was a host of things to consider: toilet facilities for an expected 200-300 people, night lighting, electrical and water hookups for RVs. The list was endless, and there was continuous brainstorming.

The reunion went splendidly. The weather cooperated. Family members came from across the country; some stayed in motels, others camped in RVs, tents and just under the stars. Every night we had a campfire. On Saturday a hog was barbecued underground. We danced later, with a family member as band-leader. The traditional meeting on Sunday was attended by 350 people, 10 times the number of the first reunion 100 years ago.

Perhaps most important, we truly did give a great deal of thought to every feature of the reunion. The goal was to anticipate _everything_. We did not hope for the best; we _planned_ for the best, but had contingency plans for the worst. Again, this was possible because we began early.

- 192 -

LEMASTER-PATTERSON

Family Reunions of Snyder, Oklahoma

We all enjoy going "back home" – a place which is associated with childhood memories; where our forebears trod and were laid to rest; where our bonds with loved ones are strengthened and renewed.

Here are some ideas and things we do at our reunions:

The **Reunion Tablecloth** (pictured above) – the family tree is embroidered in the center – individuals coming for the first time sign-in on the tablecloth – after the reunion their names are permanently embroidered onto the tree.

The **White Elephant Auction** – we have an auctioneer in the family, and every reunion we raise over $200 on our "elephants."

The **Family Cookbook** has become a treasure. We chose Circulation Services of Leawood, KS to print it. They added scads of free pages and a beautiful color cover. We included pictures of our grandparents, plus some of their old recipes.

Surprise birthday parties are fun. We also have a skit prepared by a "ham" in the group.

A bulletin board is useful, full of information, photos, cartoons, etc.

Our reunion is covered by the local newspaper and a copy of that article is reprinted in the next family newsletter.

The ALRICHES meet in Spotsylvania

Our 1st reunion was our best with 90 in attendance; the next two each fell off by half. Our best activity has been to publish history and genealogical pamphlets. A group picture taken by a professional is a must. Snapshots just don't serve the needs of the whole group.

Postcard showing the original family house in Wilmington, Delaware.

The BULLOCK Family Reunion

The Bullock Family of Parmele, North Carolina, are descendents of George Bullock Sr., who was one of seven offspring of Caesar Bullock, Sr., born into slavery in 1819.

Now our family meets each year with around 200 of our 600 members getting together from New York to North Carolina. The site and hosting of our reunion rotates among five regional committees.

We begin with an invocation and the singing of the negro hymn "Lift Every Voice and Sing." We also have a family song. We incorporate surprises into the reunion with a "Family Member of the Year Award" and birthday parties. An essay contest about the family with prizes for the children has worked well.

We ask "What does our family need?"

The family crest was designed by 16-year-old Renee Brown in 1985 and now is on T-shirts, plaques, medallions, hats, etc.

Out of this has grown the Bullock Family Scholarship Fund to assist academics. Also individual medical histories can help us trace any predisposition to illnesses.

And no reunion would be complete without the recitation of a special family poem.

Our picnic included boat rides, a hayride, and even a clown.

- One family member donated a 3-foot-wide candelabra that is now used during our memorial service and then ceremonially passed on to the group hosting next year's reunion.

Sharing long-lost photos at banquet.

POINTERS:

- Form committees to look for a site, food, entertainment, accommodations, special events, and youth activities.
- Come up with something fresh each year, a new "theme."
- Keep searching for your family — do genealogical work.
- Record the reunion well. Videotape stories and recollections to share with those who could not attend and to show future generations.

Plan a fashion show, a talent show, even a concert or an art show.

The HENSON Family Round-Up
Held at the Llano, Texas, Community Center and Rodeo Barn

At each reunion we have a calendar of all birthdays and anniversaries; genealogy books; lots of photo albums; videos & cassettes from past reunions; a "growing" cookbook; and an heirloom quilt as wall decoration.

Some Favorite Activities: Story-telling from past reunions and family experiences; gathering native wildflowers to decorate tables; playing music and singing from our songsheets; lots of games and sports — dominoes, scruples, egg toss, swimming, field trips, canoeing, etc.; birthday parties for the kids; and helping to build & update the Henson Family Tree.

Four Generation Quilt. A Henson family heirloom made by Fern Bland.

Blow-up of one panel.

Each year we have an auction with the help of a local cattle auctioneer. The families find things in attics & garages and make handcraft items to be auctioned off.

Another favorite is the "country store" where we sell lots of fun items. The kids love it and get to ring up prices on an old-fashioned cash register.

Remember: Pick a site that's good for children's play. And to quote grandfather Welborn Lee Henson, "Ask questions if you don't know the answers. No question is dumb if you don't know the answer."

Our group of 70 people stayed in condos on the beach. Condos may seem expensive but are actually quite affordable. We rented eight units (3-4 bedrooms per unit) and the total cost for three nights was $110 per person which also included two group dinners. Condos are great for reunions because they have living rooms and other areas where families can gather and visit and share meals.

A special early morning hot-air balloon ride was arranged.

Our reunion was held mid-week to save money on condominium rates but this may not be the preferred time for some in your group. It's best to get announcements out early to allow people time to make vacation plans. We started 18 months beforehand.

We sent out 5 newsletters over a period of 18 months to stimulate enthusiasm. The newsletters featured computerized clip-art such as this take-off on a traditional Japanese print. Also included were lists of things to do and places to go in the area.

The welcoming banquet was a traditional meal at a Japanese restaurant. Our BBQ at a state beach featured teriyaki chicken and fresh salmon (in foil in the photo) caught during an ocean fishing expedition by some of our group. A huge platter of sushi was part of the feast, purchased from a local restaurant.

The CONNOLLY Family Reunion
of Nova Scotia and Ontario, Canada

The Connolly Family Mini-Olympics pits Ontario vs Nova Scotia. Some of the officially approved events are:

1. egg toss
2. ski race
3. limbo stick stretch
4. basketball race
5. 3-legged race
6. obstacle course, etc.

Spot drug checking is permitted, so no steroids; no name calling; no punching; no pinching; no telling jokes to distract the other team; having fun is permitted; do laugh; yelling & screaming is encouraged; no stealing or kidnapping members of the opposite team. Points will be awarded according to the fancy of the official.

Our family has nicknames for each other and a "family dialect." Here is part of our glossary:

glasses = giglamps	carrots = rots
radio = rond-a-rurd	awful = ickbait, etc.

In the evening we have a bonfire with story-telling and "famous moments" in Connolly music.

We employed a local mentally handicapped workshop to make buttons and key chains for all the family. Good price and a good cause.

The Nova Scotia Branch of the Connolly Family Ski Team.

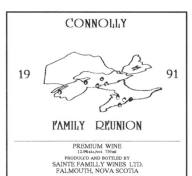

CONNOLLY

19   91

FAMILY REUNION

PREMIUM WINE
12.0% alc./vol. 750 ml
PRODUCED AND BOTTLED BY
SAINTE FAMILLY WINES LTD.
FALMOUTH, NOVA SCOTIA

We specially ordered wine from a nearby vineyard with our own label design showing a map of Nova Scotia superimposed over one of Ontario with the home towns circled.

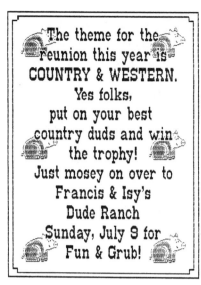

The theme for the reunion this year is
COUNTRY & WESTERN.
Yes folks,
put on your best
country duds and win
the trophy!
Just mosey on over to
Francis & Isy's
Dude Ranch
Sunday, July 9 for
Fun & Grub!

The BECK Family Reunion

As our family comes from all over the US, we asked everyone to bring "scratch-off" lottery tickets, which became the most coveted prizes for contests. We have scavenger hunts; trivia games; win, lose or draw with a large easel; soft ball; balloon tosses (always popular on hot sunny days). The kids love to guess how many pennies or M&Ms are in a jar.

We ask people to bring baby pictures and graduation photos. We then make a photo display and have people guess who is who. This year's hit was story-telling in front of a video camera — stories of growing up.

Site: Family farms are where we first had our reunions — fresh, home-grown vegetables, and the kids loved the new farm animals.

Every reunion is followed with a newsletter. We even have friends who want to become honorary family members so they can come to our reunions.

Lisa dressed as a '60s hippie. Other themes: Polynesian, Monte Carlo/ Las Vegas, wild & crazy, country & western, etc.

Each year our expert kite designers bring us new high-flyers.

The Schubin Family (687 strong) gather to celebrate a 50th Wedding Anniversary at Lincoln Center in New York City.

The SCHUBIN Family Reunion

Our immigrant family has 9 major branches. At the reunion each branch had a different color for its chart and matching label dots for name tags. Interrelated family members had several dots allowing cousins to seek each other out. We encouraged people to bring old photos, letters, and especially their children.

With such a large gathering, one problem we had was in not identifying family members in the photos as they were taken — quite difficult to do later on.

Examining composite family charts posted on the windows of Philharmonic Hall at Lincoln Center.

Through our research we found almost 600 families on 5 continents, and published a "Genealogical History of the Extended Family" — which along with Schubin, included the Erteschik, Greenberg, Klein, Kornfeld, Pencak, Racker & Weil families. We were advised by the Jewish Family Heritage Society that this was the first international Jewish family gathering in the US of this scope.

Also in 1991 we had a family reunion trip to visit our "roots" in Gorlice, Poland, and to Israel.

The Coberly Tradition

Our 1991 family reunion was held in Amana, Iowa. Approximately 190 people came — mostly from the midwest, but some from Washington and California. Any Coberly clan member was invited — no matter how they spelled the name, from Cubberly to Koberleigh. The Name came from the Cotswolds in England with a village there still called Coberly.

As people arrived we had them sign their names in a numbered guest book. This made it easy to give door prizes by just putting numbered pieces of paper into a fishbowl. Very simple. Many prizes were donated (like the family cross-stitch pictured above), so lots of folks went home with a "freebee."

Of special interest to newer clan members were the several family trees, each representing a different branch. They're drawn on boards and are over 5 feet tall.

We publish "The Coberly Tradition" twice yearly to keep our folks connected with family and reunion information. We plan reunions every two years with locations often chosen for their special outside interests: museum exhibits, galleries, etc. And do remember to prepare entertainment for the children.

The HERNANDEZ Family Reunion

Many years ago my father, Antonio Hernandez, migrated to Southern California from Guadalajara in his native Mexico. Today he and his siblings' descendents meet yearly in a park near San Fernando for a day-long picnic.

Well over 100 family members come from all over (Tijuana in the South to San Jose in the North).

When my cousin Letitia, and I (Gabriel Hernandez) got together a few years ago, we found we really did not know our family. But the idea of a family

Titino, a Spanish-speaking clown, paints youngsters' laughing faces.

reunion was a hard sell because people said we already get together a lot. But not the **whole** family. So we created a family support system to start the reunion.

A committee agreed that the food would be potluck and that individual families would share the other costs — soft drinks, T-shirts, children's entertainment, and so on. Some ideas were ruled out, like hiring a mariachi band, because we decided we wanted to be our own entertainment.

What matters to us is that the reunion helps reinforce our commitment to family in an American culture of increasingly broken homes and fragmentation.

During the picnic we had a pie-eating contest, volleyball, soccer, sack race, pass the hat contest, water balloon toss, and much more.

The STREBE Family Reunion

Helen Strebe Shriver with the European guests, Eduard and Gonda Strebe.

In 1985 our family had little information concerning our German roots. Strebe was an uncommon name. With the opening of the East and West German border our curiosity intensified. In 1990 a family member traveling in Europe made contact with an individual sharing our ancestor's name – Edward Strebe. He also had a great interest in Strebe genealogy. Much correspondence led him and his wife to be invited to attend our 1991 Strebe Family Reunion. It would be their first trip to the United States.

This news was quickly circulated and helped make this reunion something special indeed.

Activities and Displays: Our first 3 reunions were kept simple, due to inexperience and cost. We sat in a large outdoor circle, shared information and played music. Some problems: rainy weather, hearing each other, and disorganized children's activities.

For this 1991 reunion we rented indoor space with video equipment, display tables and chairs, a podium with audio equipment, easels with paper tablets. We displayed genealogical information, photo albums of past reunions, a US map with home locations, quilts, photos of our ancestor, and a hand-painted family tree.

We also had information on the pitifully neglected East German church where our ancestor had been

- 204 -

confirmed. To raise money to help restore the church, we held an auction and a raffle at the reunion. Our European guest agreed to get the funds to the church. This project gave us all a sense of pride and history.

Sites: State parks with full accommodations and outdoor activities have been chosen for all our reunions. The children loved the organized games, swims, frisbee throws, horse-back riding, hiking, boating — the list goes on and on.

Potential Problems and Tips: At most parks, you must register and pay ahead of time for your outdoor space. When reunion day arrives, make sure you have your paid receipt showing the facility number. This eliminates any static from "pavillion poachers".

If you have a buffet, make sure to set up a serving order, otherwise you'll have nothing but chaos.

Group Picture of WHAT NOT TO DO. A professional photographer would be a wise investment. Set a definite time for group pictures. We have not done this and consequently our pictures have been very poor. They even looked chaotic with quilts hanging about in disarray and chairs scattered around in front.

JUNKINS FAMILY ASSOCIATION
of Aston, PA

We held our 1991 reunion in NW Ohio in a public county park surrounded by cornfields. Lapel nametags were given to everyone. Two self-styled genealogists had family-tree printouts to inspect and add to.

A county historical museum was located adjacent to the park and proved very interesting to all. We also toured local family farms and a cemetery with many grave markers of revered ancestors.

We came across this roadsign (at left) on one of our trips. For us, "roots" activities provided a common bond for folks — some strangers to each other.

Family archaeological digs are being worked on around New England. With the help of professionals, these projects bring family members much more in contact with

their roots, and give people great projects to work on season after season. Gravestones in old family plots have been found, unearthed, and reset.

Our meals were prepared by the ladies of a local church. Such groups are especially great for this sort of thing. They are inexpensive, sincere, and completely reliable.

ADDITIONAL TIPS

- A Family Crest, Coat-of-Arms, or a Tartan. Any tradition (heraldry, dances, clothing styles, beliefs, old traditional recipes, etc.) can help bring people together, and can help in finding others.

- Buttons or Badges can be made for everyone, and even personalized with images important to that person.
- A Songbook of family songs from childhood can be a big hit and bring everyone together around a campfire.

- Musical entertainment can be great fun at a reunion.

MORE TIPS

- Remember, Birthday & Surprise Parties are a big hit. Hayrides, too. And Scavenger Hunts.
- Keepsakes — If anyone in the family has handicraft or woodcrafting skills, they might be asked to make something special for families to take home — quilt pieces, a wooden box, potpourri, etc.
- The Holl family created a large Crossword Puzzle full of family information. They also put together a Family Trivial Pursuit.
- Many families strongly suggest having a professional photographer take the group photo or family portraits.
- It's easy to get lost while out hiking or exploring, so use an experienced guide who knows the local trails.
- Set up a "Family Bank Account" to help members who have had fires, injuries or disasters.
- Rent a big canopy to guard against rainy weather & to provide shade.
- Wheelchairs are handy, just in case.
- Remember to keep pets on a leash.

Acknowledgements - Thanks to these individuals for their contributions to this Family Reunion Scrapbook:

Ilene Jones & Carol Wilson of the Dahler Family; Fern Bland & Marjorie Bland Sayles of the Henson Family; Alan Junkin & Richard C. Pugh of the Junkins Family; Christine Connolly & Thelma Bliss of the Connolly Family; Raymond & John Crinklaw; June Van Dusen Smith of the Strebe Family; Phyllis Patterson Rhodes of the Lemaster-Patterson Family; William Alrich; Tom & Virginia Ewing of the Stevens Family; Jill Keener & Peggy Ann Beck of the Beck Family; Robert H. Hallstead; Margaret Schofeld; Priscilla Clark; Mary Burkholder of the Coberly Family; Naomi Schubin Greenberg of the Schubin Family; Louise Weldy of the Holl Cousins Reunion; Robert A. Leunig; Dr. Bruce Hasegawa; Gabriel Hernandez; and Sheila L. Linton of the Bullock Family.

ABOUT the AUTHORS

Barbara Eymann Brown became interested in reunions when she collaborated with Tom Ninkovich to organize several reunions for the YMCA Camp they both attended in their youth (Camp Gaines, Sequoia Lake, California). The excitement and appreciation generated by these reunions inspired her to organize other reunions and edit an annual family newsletter, *The Eymann Family News*.

A former teacher, Barbara works as a training designer, writer, editor, videographer, and mail-order bookstore director for Performance Learning Systems, a teacher education firm. Part of her job is to write college course manuals for teachers. She also has owned a retail clothing business for 21 years. She authored "Reunion Special: Finding New Ways to Strengthen Family Ties," in *People Finder Magazine* (January 1986) and has developed family trees for her family and her husband's family.

She lives with her husband, Phil, and son, Tor, in the Sierra Nevada Mountains east of Sacramento. She can be contacted through Reunion Research, 3145 Geary Blvd. #14, San Francisco, California, 94118.

Tom Ninkovich has been collecting reunion information since 1971, and in 1982 founded Reunion Research, a company that publishes guidebooks for reunion planners, and information for the reunion market.

He is author of *Reunion Handbook: A guide for school reunions,* co-author of *Military Reunion Handbook.* and has had a column published in *Reunions Magazine.* He has been advising and teaching about reunion planning since 1982 and serves as a media and demographic resource on the subject.

He lives in the Sierra Nevada Mountains of California between Sequoia and Yosemite National Parks. His hobbies are folklore, traditional music, and backpacking. He can be contacted through Reunion Research, 3145 Geary Blvd. #14, San Francisco, California, 94118.

Please be on our... unique mailing list.

——————————————►

Dear Reunion Planner:

Many businesses offer special discounts and services to reunion planners. Being on our mailing list puts you in touch with these businesses. Why pay more than necessary for T-shirts, family cookbooks, customized videos, embroidered family crests or other special items for your family reunion? Learn about special airfares, discounts on accommodations, special ways to fund-raise for your family, and much more?

You will NOT be innundated with mail. You will prob-ably receive anywhere from 5 to 20 pieces of mail per year from businesses that can save you money or can offer you something special for your next reunion. **You can remove yourself from the list at any time.**

Inclusion on this list will help you become better informed which, in turn, will help you create better and more rewarding reunions for your family.

Many happy reunions to you.

Tom

Tom Ninkovich

☑ **Yes, please include me on a list of family reunion planners.**

Name_____

Address_____

City _____State_____Zip_____

> *The following questionnaire will help us to better serve your needs and will help to eliminate unwanted mail.*

Approximately how many people attend your reunions? _____
How often do you have reunions? _____
If you are planning your first reunion, please check here: ☐
Have you scheduled your next reunion? _____   When? _____
       Where?_____

PLEASE CHECK YOUR AREAS OF INTEREST:

☐ Discounted hotel/motel rates: *To receive information from hotels, you must list the cities or areas you are considering for future reunions:*_____

☐ Discounted travel rates   ☐ Discounted rental car rates   ☐ Family cruises
☐ Imprinted or Fund-raising items: *Circle your interests: cookbooks, cups & glassware, paperweights, embroidered patches, decals, coasters, pens & pencils, other:*_____
☐ Ways of creating better newsletters/mailers
☐ Commercial name tags/buttons
☐ Custom-designed reunion T-shirts/caps
☐ Imprinted items for decorating (balloons, napkins, banners, etc.)
☐ Family crests   ☐ Information on how to find people   ☐ Computer software
☐ Professional photography in your area, ☐ videography
☐ Ways of documenting your family history: *Circle your interests: a family history book, family video, audio tape, photos, scrapbooks, time capsules, other:*_____
☐ A magazine on reunion planning

Is there a particular item or service you are looking for that you can't find?_____

Return this form to:
Reunion Research, 3145 Geary Blvd #14, San Francisco, CA 94118.

CUSTOMIZED CROSSWORD PUZZLES

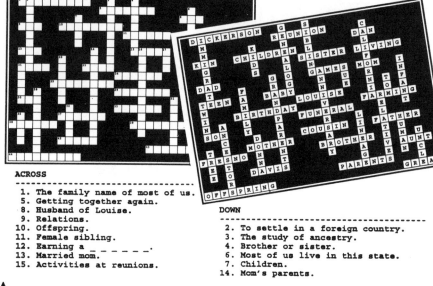

ACROSS
----
1. The family name of most of us.
5. Getting together again.
8. Husband of Louise.
9. Relations.
10. Offspring.
11. Female sibling.
12. Earning a _ _ _ _ _ _.
13. Married mom.
15. Activities at reunions.

DOWN
----
2. To settle in a foreign country.
3. The study of ancestry.
4. Brother or sister.
6. Most of us live in this state.
7. Children.
14. Mom's parents.

A crossword puzzle will really dress up your next newsletter or mailer. Or pass it around at your next reunion—maybe have a contest to see who finishes it first.

Here's how it works:
Send us a list of 50 words relating to your family (please print or type). _OR_ Send us a shorter list and we will fill it out to 50 words using common family-oriented words such as "mother," "cousin," "kin," "ancestor," etc.

The puzzle is randomly generated by computer, so some words may not be used (usually only 4–6 are left out). However, you can designate up to 5 words to be used for sure. These words will _not_ be left out. Either circle or underline these words on your list. (Remember to print or type the list.)

Then make up a clue for each word. Clues are easier to create than you might think. Short ones are better. Limit of 70 characters per clue (including spaces between words).

We will send you back a blank puzzle, a list of clues, and, of course, the solution. Then just paste it into your next newsletter or mailer. Or pass it around at your next reunion.

> **All this for only $19.95. Allow 4 weeks for delivery.**
> **Add $10 for rush orders.**

Send your list of words (50 or as many as you can think of that pertain to your family), a clue for each word, and the check to:

Reunion Research, 40609 Auberry Rd, Auberry, CA 93602.
Make checks out to "Reunion Research."

IMPORTANT: Include your deadline and phone number.

Reunion Resources
——— Products and Services ———

We pay close attention to any product or service that would benefit reunion planners, noting in particular the quality, accuracy, and reputation of the product or business involved. Many of these items and services are mentioned in the Appendix; some are offered for sale on the next few pages. If you have comments, complaints, or praises regarding any of the products or services mentioned in this book, please let us know. Also, **please bring to our attention any new items or services that, in your estimation, should be included here.**

LifeStories Board Game

We never thought we'd be selling a game, but this one is just right for family reunions. *LifeStories* is a fun game where you talk about your experiences from the past. Both young and old have such experiences, and this is a great game for mixing the ages.

Remember the kids you grew up with? Your favorite family dinner? A time when you were really lucky? A special vacation? Big and small events shape our lives and are fun to share with others. Recall funny moments, important times, and cherished thoughts. Pass on family history.

LifeStories is designed to build closer relationships among players. And best of all, everyone wins! For 2 to 8 players, ages 6 to 106. Children over 10 like to play as a group; younger children enjoy the game best when played with adults. $29.95 plus shipping. See order form, p. 215.

The Book Store

Fun & Games for Family Gatherings by Adrienne Anderson. This book gives 235+ ideas of what to do at family reunions. Games, skits, puzzles, songs, lots more. *Every reunion planner should have this book.* $12.95.

Family Associations: Organization and Management by Christine Rose, tells you why and how to go about forming a family association. Includes sample by-laws. New 2nd edition. $12.95.

Editing Your Newsletter by Mark Beach. Your reunion announcements and newsletters are what sell the reunion. Make them the best they can be. This is the only book you will ever need to create great looking newsletters and flyers. All aspects of newsletters are covered, not just editing. $22.95.

How to Outlive Your Lifetime by Tim Polk. This book carefully explains that preserving your family history now will win you a place in the hearts of your ancestors years from now. Then it shows you how. $10.95.

Reunion Handbook: For school reunions by Tom Ninkovich. Special sections on how to find people, publicizing the event, fund-raising, planning a program— all aspects are covered. *Note: This book is out-of-print but should be available soon under the new title* School Reunion Handbook. *Write for price and availability.*

ORDER FORM

IMPORTANT: If this book is more than 3 years old (see front), write for an updated price before ordering.

Name_____

Address_____

City_____State_____Zip_____

*NOTE: Committee Discount, *save $4 per book.*

ITEM	PRICE	AMOUNT
Family Reunion Handbook, first book....	$14.95	$_____
Family Reunion Handbook, for each additional book...........	10.95	_____
Fun & Games for Family Gatherings......	12.95	_____
Family Associations: Organization and Management...............	12.95	_____
How to Outlive Your Lifetime	10.95	_____
LifeStories, family board game.........	29.95	_____
Shipping for one item.................	2.50	_____
Shipping for each additional item......	1.50	_____

```
                          Sub Total.........  _____
† For Priority Mail add $2 more per item........  _____
   California residents add current sales tax...  _____
                          Grand Total.......... $_____
```

* NOTE: We will ship to multiple addresses at no additional charge. Please enclose an address list. Also, if you are buying the book as a gift, we will enclose a gift card if you like. Please indicate how to make out the card.

† Books will be shipped 4th Class Book Rate unless Priority is paid for.

Unconditional guarantee: If you are not satisfied with any item for any reason, please return it within 10 days for a full refund.

Make checks payable to: Reunion Research
Reunion Research, 3145 Geary Blvd. #14, San Francisco, CA 94118

◆ **To be on our mailing list, you must fill out the form on p. 211.**

216

Notes

APPENDIX

A listing of useful resources for reunion planners.

◆ **AWARDS, Humorous** *(Text reference: p. 91)*

• Funny Side Up, 425 Stump Rd, North Wales, PA 19454, 215/361-5142. A good source of inexpensive joke awards. In recent years, their catalog has had some items of poor taste. Be forewarned. Ask for their free catalog.

◆ **CHILDREN'S ACTIVITIES** *(Text reference: Chapters 7 and 9)*

• Animal Town, PO Box 485, Healdsburg, CA 95448, 800/445-8642, ask for their free catalog. Lots of great board games for kids and families, face painting kit, tapes, puzzles, many great books including: *Co-operative Sports and Games Book (Vols. 1 & 2); Festivals, Family and Food,* and much more.

• Chinaberry Book Service, 2780 via Orange Way #B, Spring Valley, CA 91978, 800/776-2242, 619/670-5200. "Books and music for children and families." Ask for their free catalog.

• National Association for the Preservation and Perpetuation of Storytelling (NAPPS), PO Box 309, Jonesborough, TN 37659, 800/525-4514. This association can put you in touch with a storyteller near you.

• *Awakening the Hidden Storyteller: How to build a storytelling tradition in your family* by Robin Moore. Shambhala Publications, Horticultural Hall, 300 Massachusetts Ave, Boston, MA 02115, 800/769-5561.

• *Fun & Games for Family Gatherings.* See page 214.

◆ **COMPUTER ELECTRONIC NETWORKS** *(Text reference: p. 166–67)*

• CompuServe Information Service, PO Box 20212, Columbus, OH 43220, 800/848-8199 (except Ohio) or 614/457-8600. They have a genealogy forum, and Phone*File which gives names, addresses, and phone numbers of 80 million households, nationwide. 2,000,000 members.

• GEnie Information Services, PO Box 6403, Rockville, MD 20850, 800/638-9636. Genealogy Roundtable, 30 day money-back trial.

• The National Genealogical Society maintains a BBS at 703/528-2612. Beginners should call this BBS first to get the number of the nearest genealogy BBS.

◆ **FACTS, FIGURES, and TRIVIA** *(Text reference: Chapters 5 and 14)*

Chronologies, yearly histories, old newspapers, and encyclopedia yearbooks (annual volumes) are good for finding interesting facts and gures for mailers, newsletters, and reunion programs. Your local library reference section is the place to start looking. Some good sources are:

• *The Almanac of Dates,* Linda Millgate, published by Harcourt, Brace, and Javanovich.

• *2500 Anecdotes for All Occasions,* Edmund Fuller, Dolphin Books.

• *Chronicle of the 20th Century,* edited by Clifton Daniel, Chronicle Publications, 1400 pages, newspaper format.

• *The People's Chronology,* edited by James Trager. Published by Holt, Rinehart and Winston, arranged by years, 30,000 entries, 1200+ pages. Especially good.

• *The Timetables of History,* Bernard Grun, published by Simon and Schuster, 700 page paperback. Especially good.

• *Chase's Calendar of Annual Events* by W. and H. Chase, Contemporary Books, Chicago. Source of ideas, facts, and sayings. Expensive, found in most libraries.

Historical printouts: *(Text reference: pp. 184–85)*

• Window In Time, 4321 Laurelwood Way, Sacramento, CA 95864. Send a date and get a computer printout of the history and other trivia of that time; a real value at $5 per printout (1994). However, prices may change. For the current price, send a stamped self-addressed envelope to the above address.

◆ **FAMILY ASSOCIATIONS** *(Text reference: Chapter 12)*

• *Starting and Running a Nonprofit Organization* by Joan Hummel. University of Minnesota Press, 2037 University Ave. SE, Minneapolis, MN 55455-3092. Phone orders accepted: 800/388-3863, Visa or Mastercard.

• *Family Associations: Organization and Management.* See page 214.

◆ **FAMILY HISTORY** *(Text reference: Chapter 10)*

The American Association for State and Local History, 530 Church St #600, Nashville, TN 37219, 615/255-2971, has several good books on collecting oral history. Ask for their free catalog. Among the books they have available are:

• *Oral History for the Local Historical Society,* and *Transcribing and Editing Oral History,* both by Willa K. Baum. Explains how to interview and how to transcribe, index, store, and present oral history tapes.

• *Instant Oral Biographies: How to tape record, video or film your life stories* by William Zimmerman. Guarionex Press, 201 W. 77th St, New York, NY 10024, 212/724-5259.

• *Keeping Family Stories Alive* by Vera Rosenbluth. An excellent book on how to interview family members on audio tape or video tape. Order from Hartley and Marks Publishing, PO Box 147, Point Roberts, WA 98281, 604/739-1771.

• Family History Publishers, 845 S. Main St, Bountiful, UT 84010, 801/295-7490. This company specializes in processing family histories into any desired form and then publishing them into the desired size, cover, and quantity. Send for their free brochure with instructions on "How to prepare your family history and how to get it published."

• Para Publishing, PO Box 4232, Santa Barbara, CA 93140, 800/727-2782, has many good books on paste-up, desktop publishing, and how to produce your own books. Especially recommended are *Self-Publishing Manual,* and *Publishing Short-Run Books,* both by Dan Poynter.

• Gateway Press, 1001 N. Calvert St, Baltimore, MD 21202, 410/837-8271. This company will publish your family history and/or help with various stages, such as: consulting, indexing, do-it-yourself instructions, design, pricing and marketing advice. Ask for their free brochure, "A Guide for Authors."

• "Gift of Heritage"—An instructional video from Mary Lou Productions, PO Box 17233, Minneapolis, MN 55417, 800/224-8511. Explains simple video techniques that will allow you to effectively tell your family story on video.

• "Sharing Memories"—A how-to, step-by-step computer program that allows anyone to easily record family history and memoirs. Send in your finished story (on disk) and receive a spiral bound "correction copy" of your book. Return the correction copy and get back perfect-bound 5 1/2 x 8 1/2 books of your family history and/or memoirs. Minimum order is 5 books. MS-DOS 3.0+ or Windows. Write: Sharing Memories, Box 750, Glenmoore, PA 19343, 610/458-0707.

◆ **FUND-RAISING ITEMS**

Cookbooks: *(Text reference: p. 34)*

The following printing companies specialize in creating cookbooks for fund-raisers and have how-to instructions available:

• Walter's Publishing, 215 5th Ave SE, Waseca, MN 56093, 800/447-3274, 507/835-3691. Send for free fund-raising kit.

• Circulation Service, PO Box 7306, Indian Creek Stn., Shawnee Mission, KS 66207, 800/937-6886. Send for free fund-raising kit.

• Cookbook Publishers, 10800 Lakeview, Lenexa, KS 66219, 800/227-7282, 913/492-5900. Send for their cookbook kit and price list.

• Fundcraft, PO Box 340, Collierville, TN 38027, 800/351-7822, 901/853-7070. Send for free fund-raising kit.

• Brennan Printing, 100 Main St, Deep River, IA 52222, 800/448-3740, 515/595-2000. Send for free sample and kit.

Two very nice cookbooks to see as examples are *The Black Family Reunion Cookbook* and *Black Family Dinner Quilt Cookbook* from the National Council of Negro Women, published by Wimmer Books Plus, 4210 B.F. Goodrich Blvd, Memphis, TN 38118, 800/727-1034.

Lottery tickets: *(Text reference: p. 34)*

• Scratch-It Promotions, 1763 Barnum Ave, Bridgeport, CT 06610. 800/ 966-9467, 203/367-5377. This company has "scratcher" tickets (generic or custom-made) and "scratcher" disks that you can apply to your own tickets. Invent your own scratcher fund-raiser or ask for ideas. Rush service is available.

◆ **GENEALOGY and LOCATING PEOPLE** *(Text refs.: Chaps. 10 and 13)*

• *Get the Facts on Anyone,* Dennis King. Prentice Hall/Macmillan, New York City. One of the best books available on how to find people.

• CD ROMs with names, addresses and phone numbers of 81 million people are now available at a reasonable price. Contact Digital Directory Assistance, 6931 Arlington Rd #405, Bethesda, MD 20814-5231, 800/284-8353 and ask for "PhoneDisc Residential." System requirements are IBM or compatible XT, AT, PS/2, x86, or Pentium with MSDOS 3.1+, 500K free hard disc space, 512K RAM, and CD ROM drive. Windows and Mac versions are now available.

• *Directory of Professional Genealogists,* Association of Professional Genealogists, 3421 M St. NW #236, Washington, DC 20007.

• Board for Certification of Genealogists, PO Box 5816, Falmouth, VA 22403. To locate a professional genealogist near you, write for their "Roster of Certified Persons." There is a small charge.

• National Genealogical Society, 4527 17th St. N, Arlington, VA 22207-2399, 703/525-0050. This is a membership society that offers annual conventions, a mail-order lending library, a home-study course, and many books, forms and resources for sale. To find someone near you who can speak to your group on the subject of genealogy or local history, get their "Speaker's Directory."

• The National Archives. This federal agency has available "regionally-created federal records" located in regional archives in or near Boston, New York, Philadelphia, Atlanta, Chicago, Kansas City, Fort Worth, Denver, Los Angeles, San Francisco, Seattle and Anchorage. Archive hours are generally M–F, 8–4, except federal holidays. For phone numbers, ask directory assistance for "The National Archives" in or near the cities mentioned above, or write to: The National Archives, Washington, DC 20408.

• The Family History Library of the LDS Church, 35 N. West Temple St, Salt Lake City, UT 84150, houses the most extensive collection of genealogical information in the world. Documents from around the world have been microfilmed and are available for inspection. The library is open every day except Sunday and holidays. Photcopying services, pencils and other supplies are available. To keep from being overwhelmed by the size and amount of information, send for the instructional pamphlet "A Guide to Research" which explains how to find information, gives you a library floor plan, library rules, hours, and a list of additional services. Thirty minutes spent with this pamphlet ahead of time will do wonders for your research ability, not to mention your disposition. The library information number is 801/240-2331.

The LDS Church also has over 2000 "Family History Centers" located throughout the world. These Centers are small repositories that are linked to the main library in Salt Lake City, and are good places for beginners to learn about genealogy. To locate the center nearest you, look in the white pages of your phone book under "Church of Jesus Christ of Latter Day Saints," then under that title look for "genealogy library" or "Family History Center." If that doesn't work, write to the main library in Salt Lake City (address given above).

• *Genealogical Helper Magazine,* Everton Publishers, PO Box 368, Logan, UT 84321, 800/443-6325 or 801/752-6022. Six issues per year, over 285 pages per issue—a real bargain. It will put you in direct contact with "things genealogical."

• *Heritage Quest Magazine,* PO Box 329, Bountiful, UT 84011, 801/298-5446. Another good genealogy magazine plus mail-order bookstore.

◆ **GRAPHICS SUPPLIES and BOOKS** *(Text reference: Chapters 5 and 14)*

• Dot Graphic Supply, PO Box 369, Omaha, NE 68101, 402/342-4221, 800/228-7272. Free catalog. Office Paste-Up Kit is a bare-bones set-up for under $70. Also: Lectro-Stix Waxer; Wax Stick; non-permanent spray mount adhesive; paste-up boards; clip art; Post-It Flags; paper clips; colored dots; file card signals; rub-on type; many graphics books, art and graphics supplies. The catalog gives a general idea of the tools and resources available in the trade.

• The Printers Shopper, PO Box 1056, Chula Vista, CA 91912, 800/854-2911. Free catalog. Clip art, rub-on type, borders, graphics books, clip art book of humorous certificates, art and graphics supplies, mechanical and electric paper folders, saddle stitch staplers.

• Dover Publications, 31 East 2nd St, Mineola, NY 11501, 516/294-7000. Clip art books. Ask for a catalog of their Clip Art Series.

• Graphic Products Corp, 1480 S. Wolf Rd, Wheeling, IL 60090. 708/537-9300. This company makes *Formatt,* one of the largest lines of cut-out graphic art aids. The product is available only from graphic art stores. However, the catalog, which costs at least $3 in the stores, is available free from them just for asking.

• *Editing Your Newsletter* by Mark Beach. This is the best book you can get on the subject. It covers traditional methods and using computers. Expensive but worth it. To order, see p. 214.

• *Complete Guide to Paste-up,* by Walter B. Graham, 240 pages. One of the best books on the subject. The author is the owner of Dot Graphic Supply (above). Order from them.

• Publishing Newsletters, by Howard Penn Hudson, Scribner and Sons, 866 Third Ave, New York, NY 10022. Highly recommended.

◆ **MEDICAL HISTORY** *(Text reference: p. 123)*

• March of Dimes, National Office, 1275 Mamaroneck Ave., White Plains, NY 10605, 914/428-7100, or contact your local chapter, listed in the white pages of your phone book. Ask for their free pamphlet, "Genetic Counseling."

◆ **MERCHANDISE** *(Text reference: Chapters 3 and 7)*

• Time capsules are a great way to introduce yourself (and this generation) to future generations. They can be buried or placed on the mantle. Items to include are stamps, coins, paper money, a letter to great-great-grandchildren, photos, jewelry, etc. Order from Erie Landmark Co, 4449 Brookfield Corporate Dr, Chantilly, VA 22021-1681, 800/874-7848.

• Jack Mallory serves as a consultant and source of time capsules—any use and any price. Contact him at 12258 Kirkdale Dr, Saratoga, CA 95070, 408/252-7447.

• Quality marble paperweights make great take-home gifts. You can incorporate your family crest into the design. Order from Paperweights, Ltd, 3661 Horseblock Rd, Unit "O", Medford, NY 11763, 516/345-0752.

• Customized button name tags. Order from Dot Graphic Supply, PO Box 369, Omaha, NE 68101, 800/228-7272.

• Preserve a precious photo in needlepoint or cross-stitch. Custom chart made from original photo. Designs by Karen, PO Box 65490, Vancouver, WA 98665. 360/694-6881.

• Special reunion T-shirts and caps from Reunion Research, 3145 Geary Blvd #14, San Francisco, CA 94118.

◆ **PHONE BOOKS** *(Text reference: p. 14 and p. 167)*

• *The Directory of 800 Numbers,* Consumer Edition or Business Edition.

• *The National Directory of Addresses and Telephone Numbers.* Over 200,000 listings, published and updated annually. This book may be available at your local library in the Reference Section. Among its many listings are the addresses and phone numbers of: Chambers of Commerce and convention bureaus of all major cities; Conference centers and major hotels of all major cities; Important state offices including Information Offices; County seats of every county in the U.S.

◆ **PHOTO ALBUMS and SCRAPBOOKS** *(Text reference: p. 88)*

• Exposures, PO Box 3615, Oshkosh, WI 54903, 800/222-4947. All reunion groups should keep photo albums and scrapbooks. This company has a good selection, including an Oversize Scrapbook. Free catalog.

• Enduring Memories, 7 Dogwood Ln, Willow Street, PA 17584. 717/464-0963. Albums, scrapbooks and supplies. Acid-free, archival quality. Photo labeling pencils. Free catalog.

◆ **REUNION CONFERENCES**

Temple University School of Social Administration sponsors an annual African-American Family Reunion Conference. In 1993 their sixth annual conference took place over 3 days the last week in March and cost $25 per person. Featured were speakers, panelists, exhibits, and 3 workshops with topics such as "Special Events," "Organizing and Funding," "Tracing Your Roots," and "Strengthening the Family." This is by far the most serious family reunion conference in the U.S. to date. Contact: School of Social Administration, Family Reunion Institute, Ritter Hall Annex, Temple University, Philadelphia, PA 19122.

◆ **SITE SELECTION** *(Text reference: pp. 10–12, and p. 107)*

• *Super Family Vacations: Resort and Adventure Guide,* Martha Shirk and Nancy

Klepper, HarperCollins, New York. Excellent, highly recommended.

• *Ranch Vacations* by Eugene Kilgore. Lists over 200 guest ranches in the U.S. and Canada, and includes information on children's programs, rates, and nearby attractions. Published by John Muir Publications, PO Box 613, Santa Fe, NM 87504, 800/888-7504. Order by phone with MasterCard or Visa.

• Houseboat Association of America, 4940 N. Rhett Ave, Charleston, SC 29406, 803/744-6581. Send $2 for a listing of all houseboat rental companies in the U.S. and Canada.

◆ **STATIONERY SUPPLIES** *(Text reference: Chapters 4, 5 and 6)*

• Quill Corp., 100 S. Schelter Rd, Lincolnshire, IL 60197-4700. Imprinted and plain envelopes; file card trays, metal or plastic, 3 sizes; file cards, 3 sizes, lined or plain and in 6 colors plus white; address labels.

• Walter Drake and Sons, Colorado Springs, CO 80940 (that's all the address you need). For return address labels, and imprinted envelopes in quantities of 100.

• The U.S. Postal Service can provide you with personalized stamped envelopes in quantities as low as 50, and in either regular or business size. Ask your local Post Office to send you a "Personalized Envelope Order Form" which explains the options and prices.

INDEX

About Our Advertisers

Many businesses cater to family reunions. But sometimes they are hard to find, especially when you're planning a "long-distance" reunion, or are looking for a particular supplier or a hard-to-find product. It's also hard to know which companies are making special offers aimed at the family reunion market.

The advertisers on the following pages all have something specifically designed and targeted for family reunions. Please allow them to serve you. And while you're at it, **please mention that you saw their ad in this book.**

Advertiser's Index

(listed in order of appearance)

WHO WOULD
KNOW BETTER
HOW TO

REUNITE

FAMILY AND
FRIENDS?

At Holiday Inn® hotels, we appreciate the importance of keeping in touch with family and friends, regardless of the season. And we understand that a successful reunion takes time and planning. So we've designed a planning guide to help you organize your next Family, Military or School reunion. For your free reunions planning guide, call 1-800-447-7300.

❋ Holiday Inn®
STAY WITH SOMEONE YOU KNOW.®

FOR GROUP RESERVATIONS CALL 1-800-633-8464.

Enjoy Family Values at Group Rate Prices

WASHINGTON, D.C.
Days Inn Capitol Beltway, MD
Days Inn Springfield Mall, VA

VIRGINIA
Days Inn Carmel Church
Days Inn Emporia
Days Inn Hampton
Days Inn Richmond/Airport
Days Inn Chester
Days Inn Richmond/W. Broad
Comfort Inn Richmond/W. Broad

NORTH CAROLINA
Radisson Governors Inn
Days Inn Rocky Mount
Days Inn Fayetteville-North/Wade

SOUTH CAROLINA
Days Inn Santee
Days Inn Charleston / Historic District
Days Inn Charleston / Patriot's Point
Days Inn Charleston / Airport

TENNESSEE
Days Inn Knoxville/West Lovell Rd
Comfort Inn Kingsport/Downtown

GEORGIA
Days Inn Savannah / Oglethorpe Mall

FLORIDA
Days Inn Sarasota / Airport
Days Inn Tampa / Busch Gardens-North
Days Inn Fort Myers-South / Airport

Wish You Were Here!

HORIZON
HOTELS LIMITED

For Family Reunion Packages and Rates
Call Toll Free Reservations
1-800-448-6873

COLORADO SPRINGS.

OUR ROCKY MOUNTAIN SUNSHINE

MAKES THE YEARS MELT AWAY.

Every year, thousands of people choose Colorado Springs, Colorado, as the ideal spot to get back together with friends and family they haven't seen for years.

**COLORADO SPRINGS
COLORADO**

They enjoy our breathtaking scenery. Easy access and transportation. Luxurious yet affordable accommodations. Exciting attractions and activities, from the scenery of the Rockies to the casinos of Cripple Creek. It's easy to relax and have a good time here in the shadow of Pikes Peak…and little by little, the years just seem to melt away.

It all starts when you contact the Colorado Springs Convention and Visitors Bureau's experienced reunion specialists. They'll work with you to plan a unique, unforgettable event for your group, and help you with the details, from accommodations and reservations to special events and attractions.

Call 1-800-888-4748 today and let's get together.

CALL OR WRITE FOR FREE GROUP TOUR INFORMATION
COLORADO SPRINGS CONVENTION & VISITORS BUREAU
104 S. CASCADE, SUITE 104, COLORADO SPRINGS, CO 80903
1-800-888-4748, EXT. 138 OR 135 *FAX: (719) 635-4968*
WEB SITE: http://www.coloradosprings-travel.com/cscvb/

Reunion T's and Caps

Outfit your group with the best in reunion T-shirts and caps. Use one of our special designs (send for examples), use your own, or we can create a design for you.

- Use T's and caps as fund-raisers by charging a dollar or 2 over your cost.
- *No set-up charge.*
- Minimum order as low as one dozen.
- Mix shirt colors to identify different branches of your family (no extra charge).
- Mix sizes (no extra charge).

T-shirts (one color ink on one side)

Quantity	Lightwt. 50/50*	Heavywt. 50/50	Lightwt. 100%**	Heavywt. 100%
12-99	$5.99	$6.99	$6.99	$7.99
100-288	5.59	6.59	6.59	7.59
289-499	4.49	5.49	5.49	6.49
500+ call				

*50/50 = 50% poly, 50% cotton; **100% = 100% cotton
- Sizes: XS, S, M, L, XL (larger sizes: add 99¢ per shirt)
- Almost any color cloth and any color ink is available.
- For each additional ink color add 99¢ per shirt.
- Prices are for camera-ready artwork supplied by you or for one of our special reunion designs (top, next page). If we create the design for you from your instructions, add $12 per order.
- Embroidery on caps and shirts is available. Also good prices on screen-printed sweatshirts. Call if interested.
- Shipping is extra. We ship UPS unless instructed otherwise.
- We can deliver within 4 weeks. For rush orders add $20.
- We require 100% payment before the order is shipped.

Caps (one size fits all, one ink color. For 2nd ink color add 50¢ per cap)

Quantity	Visors	Foam/mesh	Poplin	Golf
12-36	$4.99	$4.99	$6.99	$6.99
37-144	4.69	4.69	6.69	6.69
144+	4.39	4.39	6.39	6.39

To Order T-shirts or Caps—

For better service, we prefer to talk to you by phone. To initiate our T-shirt or cap services, please send us your name, address, phone number, artwork (if any) and a brief description of your needs. We will phone you to discuss your order. Send a phone number where you can be reached in the evenings or on the weekends. Or just call us at 209/855-2101 to start the process.

Reunion Research, 3145 Geary Blvd #14, San Francisco, CA 94118.

ANGEL FIRE

NEW MEXICO'S PREMIER FAMILY RESORT

The Legends Hotel & Conference Center is northern New Mexico's premier meeting facility. With more than 15,000 square feet of meeting space in eleven different conference rooms, we can accommodate groups from 25 to 500. The Legends offers 157 guest rooms, three restaurants, spa with indoor swimming pool, hot tub and exercise equipment, lounge, fine art gallery, gift shop and game rooms. Also available are a variety of resort-managed condominiums: from studios to three-bedroom units.

Angel Fire is New Mexico's premier four-season mountain resort. We offer a wide variety of summer activities and can organize fishing, golf , tennis, and volleyball tournaments. Or we can arrange scenic chair-lift rides, bar-b-ques, family picnics, as well as horseback riding and hiking excursions. And after colors of autumn have turned, so do the thoughts of Angel Fire skiers. The turning of the leaves and the first winter snows kick Angel Fire into high gear for family ski enthusiasts. We offer a variety of family ski programs that teach you to improve your skiing while having a great time together as a family.

800-633-7463

THE POCONOS
Get Away To It All.

Pocono Mountains Reunions Are Naturally Exciting.

Nature at its best with attractions galore. 2400 square miles of what it takes to make reunions memorable. Accommodations from large resorts to country inns. Let us help you pick one.

Call us for FREE planning assistance and information for your next Pocono reunion: 800/722-9199

Pocono Mountains Convention & Visitors Bureau
1004 Main St, Box 127
Stroudsburg, PA 18360

Bledsoe, Stiles, Marshal Carver . . .

They were drawn by our charming shops, fine restaurants, cozy accommodations, historic treasures and scenic hill country beauty.

They returned because of our friendly service, attention to detail and fun family atmosphere.

Call for a free family reunion planning kit.

(800) GEO-TOWN
(436-8696)

Georgetown, Texas only 25 miles north of Austin, Texas on Interstate 35.

CLASSIFIED ADVERTISING

Fun & Games for Family Gatherings describes over 235 games, activities, and ideas to make family get-togethers fun and interesting.

See pages 214 and 215 for ordering information.

GAMES: Pre-school games, pre-teen games, teen games, ethnic games, hiking games, balloon games, cross-generational games, relationship games, paper-and-pencil games, banquet games, guessing games, co-operative games.

ACTIVITIES: Programs, talent shows, skits, videography, fund-raisers, beginning genealogy, mixers, ice breakers, auctions, bake sales, family store, banquets, treasure hunts, songs, building projects, arts & crafts.

IDEAS: Fun food, registration, name tags, contests, prizes, awards, personalized items, scrapbooks, hobby displays, photo displays, memorabilia displays, ethnic themes & motifs.

CUSTOMIZED CROSSWORD PUZZLES

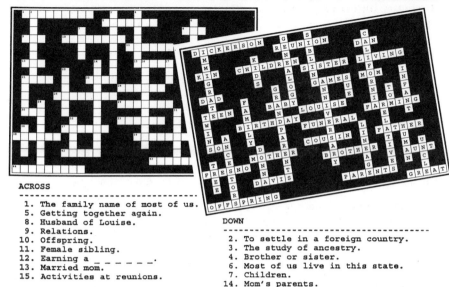

ACROSS
----
1. The family name of most of us.
5. Getting together again.
8. Husband of Louise.
9. Relations.
10. Offspring.
11. Female sibling.
12. Earning a _ _ _ _ _ _.
13. Married mom.
15. Activities at reunions.

DOWN
----
2. To settle in a foreign country.
3. The study of ancestry.
4. Brother or sister.
6. Most of us live in this state.
7. Children.
14. Mom's parents.

A crossword puzzle will really dress up your next newsletter or mailer. Or pass it around at your next reunion—maybe have a contest to see who finishes it first.

Here's how it works:

Send us a list of 50 words relating to your family (please print or type). *OR* Send us a shorter list and we will fill it out to 50 words using common family-oriented words such as "mother," "cousin," "kin," "ancestor," etc.

The puzzle is randomly generated by computer, so some words may not be used (usually only 4–6 are left out). However, you can designate up to 5 words to be used for sure. These words will **not** be left out. Either circle or underline these words on your list. (Remember to print or type the list.)

Then make up a clue for each word. Clues are easier to create than you might think. Short ones are better. Limit of 70 characters per clue (including spaces between words).

We will send you back a blank puzzle, a list of clues, and, of course, the solution. Then just paste it into your next newsletter or mailer. Or pass it around at your next reunion.

> **All this for only $19.95. Allow 4 weeks for delivery.**
> **Add $10 for rush orders.**

Send your list of words (50 or as many as you can think of that pertain to your family), a clue for each word, and the check to:

Reunion Research, 40609 Auberry Rd, Auberry, CA 93602.
Make checks out to "Reunion Research."

IMPORTANT: Include your deadline and phone number.

Free Reunion Checklist Guide

Whether you're planning a reunion for five or five hundred your best bet for getting everyone together is Best Western's Together Again reunion program. Reunion Professionals will provide you with a free reunion kit, including the **Reunion Checklist Guide**. We'll even help you with everything from invitations to personalized T-shirts. Call today for more information. And see why we're the "long time no see" specialists.

Your Best Bet Is A Best Western
For reservations call 1-800-528-1234